BLEND - 2: SOFTWARE INFRASTRUCTURE

W. P. DODD and T. I. MAUDE

Library and Information Research Report 58

Peter Dodd graduated in Physics from the University of Birmingham and was then involved in research into elementary particle physics, working at Birmingham, Brookhaven, and C.E.R.N. He subsequently moved into Computer Science and is currently a senior lecturer in Computer Science, and deputy director of the Computer Service at the University of Birmingham.

Tim Maude graduated in Mathematics from the University of Bath and obtained an MSc. in Computer Science at Birmingham, before being appointed as Research Associate on the BLEND project. He is now employed at British Telecom Research Laboratories.

Library and Information Reports are
published by the British Library and distributed by the British Library Publications Sales Unit, Boston Spa, Wetherby, West Yorkshire, LS23 7BQ, UK. In the USA and Canada they are distributed by Longwood Publishing Group Inc, 27 South Main Street, Wolfeboro, New Hampshire 03894, USA. In Japan they are distributed by Kinokuniya Co Ltd, PO Box 55, Chitose, Tokyo 156, Japan.

ISBN 0 7123 3107 7
ISSN 0263 1709

The opinions expressed in this report are those of the authors and not necessarily those of the British Library.

In an effort to publish this report quickly, it is reproduced in the form in which it was received from the authors.

Typeset by the Computer Centre, University of Birmingham and printed in Great Britain by Quorn Selective Repro Ltd.

BLEND - 2: SOFTWARE INFRASTRUCTURE

British Library Cataloguing in Publication Data

Dodd, W.P.

BLEND - 2: software infrastructure -
(Library and information research report, ISSN 0263-1709;58)
1. Electronic data processing   2.Computer software
3. Telecommunications
I. Title II.Maude, T.I.   III Series
004.2'1'019 QA76

ISBN 0-7123-3107-7

ABSTRACT

This report is one of a series describing a four-year programme jointly organised by two universities and called the Birmingham and Loughborough Electronic Network Development (BLEND). The aims were to assess the cost, efficiency and subjective impact of an electronic communication system, and to explore and evaluate alternative forms of user communication through an electronic journal and information network.

Using a host computer at the University of Birmingham, a community of about 50 scientists (Loughborough Information Network Community - LINC) was connected through the public telephone network to explore various types of communication including journals, annotated abstracts, workshops, conferences, co-operative authorship, etc. Following this start in 1981, five other communities have been using the system for these various types of electronic communication. Included in this report is a brief overview of the experiment but the primary content is description of the software and telecommunications system used to support the experimental programme. One of the first decisions of the project team was to base the software on an existing computer teleconferencing system rather than produce a new software suite. This permitted an earlier start to the experimental programme, and allowed expansion of the software to meet needs as they were uncovered, rather than attempting to anticipate potential needs.

The basic teleconferencing system was enhanced in a number of ways during the course of the study, and the reasons for these enhancements and the process whereby they were incorporated and monitored is fully described.

Throughout the project relevant data has been gathered to enable the assessment of system and user performance, cost, usefulness and acceptability. These results form the contents of further reports in this series.

CONTENTS

LIST OF FIGURES

ACKNOWLEDGEMENTS

The research programme was funded by the British Library Research and Development Department and was carried out jointly by the Centre for Computing and Computer Science at the University of Birmingham and the HUSAT Research Group, Department of Human Sciences, Loughborough University of Technology.

In addition to the main authors, the following people at Loughborough and Birmingham have contributed directly to the research presented in this report:

Loughborough University of Technology: Professor B.Shackel, Mr. D. J. Pullinger

University of Birmingham: Dr. J. L.Schonfelder (now at University of Liverpool)

Throughout the study there has been much help and encouragement from Professor Peter Jarratt, Director of the Centre for Computing and Computer Science, University of Birmingham, and from the staff of the Centre, especially Mr. C. Amos, Mr. B. Bracher, Ms. B. Hall, Mr. M. Hewitt and Dr. P.Ramsay.

Finally we wish to thank the secretarial staff in the Centre (Ms. M. Deeley, Ms. J. Heathcote, Ms. P. Hurd, and Ms. S. Oliver) who have helped in the preparation of this report and throughout the project.

PROJECT AIMS

The aims of the programme were to explore and evaluate forms of user communication through an 'electronic journal' and information network, and to assess the cost, efficiency and subjective impact of such a system.

In order to accomplish these aims, the following seven main steps were taken:

1. Setting up a host computer system (BLEND).
2. Setting up a group of users (LINC).
3. Setting up electronic journals.
4. Developing the system.
5. Introducing other groups of users to the system.
6. Analysing and evaluating the system and groups of users.
7. Appraisal.

A series of reports describe the work:

BLEND - 1: Background and Development.
BLEND - 2: Software Infrastructure.
BLEND - 3: The 'Electronic Journal' Research.
BLEND - 4: User-System Interaction.
BLEND - 5: The Computer Human Factors Journal.
BLEND - 6: The References, Abstracts and Annotations Journal.
BLEND - 7: Other Studies and User Communities.
BLEND - 8: Cost Appraisal.
BLEND - 9: Overview and Appraisal.

The scope of these reports is summarised in the following Table.

REPORT SUBJECT	BLEND-1 BACKGROUND & DEVELOPMENT	BLEND-2 SOFTWARE INFRASTRUCURE	BLEND-3 THE 'ELECTRONIC JOURNAL' RESEARCH	BLEND-4 USER-SYSTEM INTERACTION	BLEND-5 THE COMPUTER HUMAN FACTORS JOURNAL	BLEND-6 THE 'REFERENCES ABSTRACTS & ANNOTATIONS JOURNAL'	BLEND-7 OTHER STUDIES AND USER COMMUNITIES	BLEND-8 COST APPRAISAL	BLEND-9 OVERVIEW AND APPRAISAL
1 Background	Background to project		Background to electronic journals	Background in relationship to development of area of Human Computer Interaction			BLEND as a test-bed		
2 Setting up a host computer system (BLEND)	Choice of software Initial development	Birmingham DEC 20 Choice of software Initial development Telecommunications required						Cost analysis	
3 Setting up a group of users	LINC and its first 3 years			Pre-BLEND questionnaires and interviews Working habits of LINC members					
4 Setting up journals	Different types of communication, development of RAAJ and presentation of CHF		Different types of journal, bulletins. newsletters, etc Journal editorial procedure. Handling refereeing. etc.			Development of of RAAJ			
5 Development of BLEND system	Software development, general description	How software development was accomplished by prototyping. Further software facilities and development. BLEND system administration and maintenance	Presentation of text for reading journals on-line	Phone surveys after after 6 months and 35 months		Software for RAAJ			
6 Other groups of users introduced to system	List of other groups of users and what they are doing		Journals for other groups of users				User communities and related studies		
7 Use of BLEND system —									
7.1 Analysis and attitude survey		Performance of the DEC 20, the software and its use. Evaluation of software specially developed.	Journal use and procedure. Description of reading and writing on/for BLEND	Post-BLEND Questionnaires Working habits of LINC members. satisfaction and Task Match		Journal use and and procedure	TORCH studies	Cost analysis	
7.2 Contents of BLEND			Listing of different types and structures		Contents of the CHF journal	Short Contents of of the RAAJ journal			
8 Future developments and proposals based on learning from BLEND.		Future software							

Table of the Contents of BLEND Reports

1. Background and Introduction to the BLEND Study

This report is one of a series describing various aspects of a research programme financed by the British Library Research and Development Department (BLR&DD) from September 1980 until September 1984. This programme was originally entitled the 'electronic journal project' and has more recently been termed the BLEND project as the aims of the project were wider than those implied by the earlier title.

Because the study has involved people from a number of different disciplines, and because the electronic journal has itself generated a large number of papers not directly related to the study, a decision was made to issue a number of reports each dealing with one particular aspect of the study. The present report is, as its title implies, concerned with the software support system that was used and developed over the four years. It will also discuss various aspects of telecommunications related to the project, and will make some suggestions for future development. However, because we do not anticipate that all readers will have access to the complete range of reports, this chapter contains a brief overview of the project, its rationale, its development and its achievements.

1.1 Background

The motivation for the study lies in the intersection of a problem and a technology that may possibly alleviate the problem. The problem concerns the production of learned journals for which the last decade has seen steadily rising costs and increasing production delays. The rising costs have been partially caused by the labour intensive nature of conventional publishing which might involve numerous re-typings of each article from the time that it is conceived by the author until it reaches the reader. This re-typing also partially explains the production delays, but these can also be caused by the time taken in the editorial processing, especially the formal refereeing of each article, and in the printing queues.

These rising costs have, usually, been passed on to the subscriber, and because there have also been financial restrictions, especially on institutional libraries, this combination has led to a decrease in circulation, which has in its turn led to an increase in unit costs, and so on. In a recent report by the Royal Society (1981) it was suggested that, for these reasons, the scientific information service, which has been taken for granted for so long, can no longer be regarded as stable.

1

An inevitable outcome of this is that sections of the community are increasingly isolated from primary material, or need to suffer even greater delays as the material, even after publication, must be requested from one of the regional or national centres, such as the Lending Division of the British Library. This is all happening at a time when the necessity for a multidisciplinary approach is being encountered in a number of research areas.

Some partial alleviation of the problem is offered by the on-line bibliographic databases, such as BLAISE, and research programmes such as the DOCDEL projects sponsored by DG XIII of the Commission of the European Communities (C.E.C). However, these approaches address only part of the problem, and certainly do not alter the increasing isolation felt by the individual worker whose principal contact with other workers in the same field is now through database searches, photocopies of articles, and occasional participation in increasingly expensive conferences and workshops.

In other fields also, the cost of attending conferences and meetings is becoming prohibitively expensive, not only in the direct costs of travel and accommodation but in the indirect costs of travel time, reduced efficiency resulting from jet-lag and absence from the normal working environment with its support service and works of reference. Technological solutions to some of these problems have given rise to the concept of teleconferencing in which conference delegates or committee members communicate with each other using either multiway telephone hook-ups (audio-teleconferencing), closed circuit television links (video-teleconferencing) or, more recently, multiple access computer systems (computer teleconferencing).

Computer teleconferencing grew out of early use of such computer systems as message-switching facilities. Operating systems would allow one user to send a message to a colleague who happened to be using the computer at the same time. This was soon extended to a facility, now known as electronic mail, whereby the message could be retained within the computer memory until the next time the colleague used the machine. Messaging was no longer a synchronous Activity, and people working overnight or late into the evening could leave messages for their colleagues working more conventional hours, and expect a reply when they next logged in.

The potential of such messaging became even more apparent with the introduction of combined computing and telecommunication systems. Users were no longer required to work in close proximity to the computer, but could access it over conventional telephone lines from anywhere in the world. This extended the use of computers as mailbox facilities and necessitated a structured approach. One such approach is that of computer teleconferencing in which messages can be sent either to individuals or to groups, and the messages can be arranged according to topic. In order that all members of the group have an opportunity to read the messages, these must be retained in the computer memory, usually for some considerable time. It is therefore little problem to retain such messages "for ever" and so build up a full record of the communication so that previous messages can be recalled using search techniques as and when the need arises.

The early research in computer teleconferencing began at the Augmentation Research Laboratory of Stanford Research Institute, at the Institute for the Future, and at New Jersey Institute of Technology. From this early work, computer conferencing is now well established as a medium to aid commercial, scientific and technical work (cf Hiltz & Turoff, 1978; Johansen, Vallee & Spangler, 1979; Vallee, 1984). Computer conferencing aids participants to communicate with each other mainly in an informal way, but it was not long before the suggestion was made that this medium might assist or even replace the traditional form of learned publication, and in effect produce 'electronic journals'. The idea of an 'editorial processing centre' was proposed by Bamford, 1976, and Woodward et al., 1976, whereby a number of learned societies might form a co-operative editorial office with the tasks of the editors and referees being facilitated by modern technology in the form of electronic mail, and articles for publication being in machine-readable form, e.g. on magnetic tape or floppy-disc. The objective of the editorial processing centre was partly to minimise costs by reducing re-typing, but the concept could be taken a stage further so that the delivered journal might also be available 'on-line'. This is what is meant by the electronic journal.

The first research project (Sheridan et al., 1981) into the study of electronic journals was funded by the US National Science Foundation and was operational from October 1976 to March 1980. Within the general programme the electronic equivalent to the traditional refereed journal was studied for a period of 18 months (October 1978 to March 1980). This study was confined to North America, for although a British participation had been anticipated, this was prevented by a British Post Office embargo on extensive transatlantic computer-based message transmission.

The Sheridan/Senders study gained some useful insights into group communication via this relatively new medium although it did not achieve its aims with regard to the refereed journal. The reasons for this are discussed in the final report (Sheridan et al., 1981), and are summarised in Figure 1.1. However, in view of the potential importance of electronic journals, especially with regard to the rising costs of materials, production, publishing and library facilities (for further discussion see Senders, 1977; Lancaster, 1978; Meadows, 1980), and because of the lack of British involvement in the North American study, the British Library Research and Development Department decided that it would be desirable to further explore the concept of the electronics journal by establishing another project in the UK. Professor N.Moray, who had previously applied to join the NSF-funded project, recommended Professor Brian Shackel (of the Human Sciences Department, University of Technology, Loughborough) as a possible director, and consequently an application was invited and after due negotiation the programme was established from June 1980.

1.2 The Blend Project

The development towards the British project started with its emphasis upon a refereed papers journal, and while that remained the starting point the initial proposal recommended exploring various other uses of the electronic communication system. The belief was that it was possible to amalgamate the less formal aspects of communication between scholars working in the same area with the more formal 'journal' aspects. There are many ways whereby such people share information, and it can be argued that exchanges over coffee during breaks in face-to-face conferences are just as important as the formally presented papers.

These various levels of communication are summarised in Figure 1.2 and the aims of the programme were to explore and evaluate the use of an electronic communication network as an aid to writing, submitting and refereeing papers, and within the same basic structure to study the use of the medium for the other levels of scholarly communication.

The first stage of the study was to make operational an acceptable software and communication system, and then to evaluate the use of this system using a number of different communities. For reasons to be discussed in the next chapter, Professor Shackel and BLR&DD approached the Centre for Computing and Computer Science at the University of Birmingham to see whether they would be willing

4

1. Too many projects and users on EIES, resulting in variable and often long system response delays.

2. Command structure and editing system too complex for 'computer naive' users.

3. Lack of flexibility in journal procedure (e.g. only on-line input permitted, and absolute assignment of copyright required).

4. Lack of status or prestige for a hitherto unpublished 'journal' probably gave it low priority for potential authors.

5. Quality and flexibility of terminals too limited in relation to possible benefits for users (it is easy to forget how much terminals have improved since 1977-78).

6. Little use of techniques to increase involvement of user community (e.g. face-to-face meetings).

7. Project duration (18 months) probably too short.

Fig 1.1:   Problems with the 1978-80 USA Refereed Papers Journal

```
Refereed Paper Journals                    Formal
Bulletins                                     ▲
Conference Proceedings                        │
Conference papers (spoken)                    │
Pre-publication draft circulation             │
Seminars                                      │
Work messages                                 ▼
Chit-chat                                   Informal
```

Fig 1.2:   Some of the different communication
            modes in a scientific community

to participate in the study, with Birmingham providing and developing the software and hardware facilities and Loughborough setting up and evaluating the user communities. This collaboration became known as the Birmingham and Loughborough Electronic Network Development (BLEND).

During the course of the project there have been, and still are, a number of communities making use of BLEND, and details of these are given in other reports in this series; however, it was only in one of these communities that the full potential of the system was explored. This was the first of the communities and consisted of people active in the field of Computer Human Factors. This was the area of Professor Shackel's own speciality, and as he had previously acted as editor of a print-on-paper journal in this area it was felt that he could bring his experience to bear and that this would also allow some direct comparisons between the two media to be made. Professor Shackel therefore acted as initial organiser and journal editor for this community, which became known as the Loughborough Information Network Community (LINC), and Mr. David Pullinger was appointed to the project to provide user support, but primarily to act as project evaluator.

Within the LINC study, the participants agreed to write a number of articles per year which could either be submitted to the journal editor for formal refereeing, or made available to the other members of the group as pre-publication drafts, or Poster Papers. The former route made it possible to study the refereeing procedure, while the latter allowed an early evaluation of the problems associated with the on-line access of lengthy pieces of text. However, the initial aim was to create a community spirit within the group, and this was encouraged by the use of BLEND in its less formal aspect, and by a preliminary face-to-face meeting at which the aims of the project and its methodology were discussed.

The experimental period for the LINC community lasted for about 3 1/2 years, during which time four issues of the refereed journal were produced, and together with the non-refereed sections there were 88 papers altogether. Additionally a number of more specialised computer teleconferences were held on various topics relating to group interests.

One particularly successful component of the LINC study was the development of an Abstracts Journal, again in the field of Computer Human Factors. One interesting feature of the new medium is the relative ease with which it is possible to annotate the formal abstracts with individual comments, such as one might obtain from a colleague, regarding the merits of each article. In this way it is possible to build up a database of references not only of interest to oneself, but known to be highly regarded by one's colleagues, or especially by those whose judgement one trusts.

When the LINC community was well underway, and when the initial system had been made more acceptable, a number of other communities were introduced to BLEND. One of these was based on the Library Schools in the UK who were given read-only access to the more formal material in the LINC project; the other groups had their own information base. Of the three principal groups, one was based on a research network for further education colleges (FERN); one was part of the programme for microelectronics education in schools (MACE); and the third developed when, with the commencement of the Alvey programme, we decided to mount the *Alvey Newsletter* in BLEND and to provide facilities for discussion between readers of the newsletter. These groups are discussed in some detail in the other reports.

2. THE INITIAL SOFTWARE

2.1 Selection

The preparatory work for the BLEND study commenced during the latter part of 1979, after Professor Shackel's proposal for the study of an electronic journal system had been accepted by BLR&DD. As far as the software support system was concerned, this preparatory work amounted to a decision whether to develop a new piece of software or to adapt some existing system.

The North American study referred to in Chapter 1 had taken a decision to use an existing piece of software, and this seemed a sensible course to follow for the present study. It had the advantage of providing an early start to the experimental period, and would provide a starting point if we were to develop a customised electronic journal software system. In 1979 we had no idea what such a system would look like, and any system that we developed would need to go through a prolonged series of prototypes. So we, also, decided to start part way down this road by using an existing piece of software, which we have regarded throughout as an initial testbed system.

The next decision was 'Which piece of software?', and again following the lead of the Sheridan/Senders study we decided to use a computer teleconferencing system. This had the advantage that such a system should be readily able to handle the less formal aspects of communication, which would predominate in the early stages of the study, especially while we were building up the cohesion of our experimental community. Our belief was that more formal aspects, such as a learned article, could be mapped onto the information structures provided by a computer teleconferencing system.

We departed however from the lead given by the Sheridan/Senders study in our selection of a teleconferencing system. In 1980 there were only two such systems commercially available - the Electronic Information Exchange System (EIES) developed at the New Jersey Institute of Technology (NJIT) by Murray Turoff, and the NOTEPAD system developed by Jacques Vallee and others at the Infomedia Corporation now of San Bruno, California. The Sheridan/Senders study had decided to use the EIES software package, whereas our preparatory investigation suggested that the NOTEPAD system might be more appropriate for our needs.

This decision was not taken simply out of a desire to be slightly different, though even that rationale would have had value in the early stages of the study of electronic journal systems. The differences between EIES and NOTEPAD, especially with regard to the way in which information was presented, might have led to a heightened understanding of the way in which an electronic journal could be represented. The real reasons were more concrete.

Early comments coming out of the Sheridan/Senders study suggested that EIES was slightly difficult or inconvenient to use for participants who were not experienced with computers. This finding was confirmed in the final report on that Project (Sheridan et al., 1981). Since most of our user community fell into the category, this was something we could not ignore. Visits in early 1980 to NJIT and Infomedia by Professor Peter Kirstein, University College, London, the Chairman of BLR&DD's New Technology Group, and to Infomedia by Brian Shackel, confirmed that NOTEPAD would be a simpler system for new users, though perhaps without the richness of data structure offered by EIES. However, we were of the opinion that NOTEPAD offered sufficient flexibility for our purposes, and it has the additional benefit of an extensive data collection and analysis package which could be used to study user behaviour. Moreover Infomedia agreed to provide a copy of NOTEPAD to be used locally in the UK and to make a limited number of amendments to the code if our initial use of the system suggested that this was necessary. Any other improvements made by Infomedia to NOTEPAD in the course of their own work would also be made available to us.

These arrangements seemed suitable, especially as we were to obtain NOTEPAD on a 6-month trial basis, and it is unlikely that we could have obtained a similar arrangement for EIES. We obtained our first version of NOTEPAD in August 1980 with a view to commencing the training period of our main user community in October.

2.2 The NOTEPAD Computer Teleconferencing System

NOTEPAD is a proprietary product of the Infomedia Corporation whose main interest in NOTEPAD is to provide a computer teleconferencing bureau rather than to directly market the software. In fact the BLEND Project was the first and, so far, only purchaser of NOTEPAD, and we are grateful to Infomedia, and particularly to Dr. Jacques Vallee, for their decision to relax their own rules on our behalf. We were allowed to purchase only the compiled version of the code however, which meant that we were unable to modify the software ourselves, although we were able to make some additions in ways to be described later.

Since NOTEPAD is only available for use on the DEC20 series of computers, BLR&DD and Brian Shackel approached Professor Peter Jarratt, Director of the Computer Centre at the University of Birmingham, to see whether his department would be prepared to collaborate on the research Project. Birmingham would provide the computer facility and software and telecommunications expertise, and Loughborough would provide the Human Factor expertise and manage the user community.

This arrangement was agreed upon in the Spring of 1980, with BLR&DD providing the additional finance both for the purchase of NOTEPAD and for the support of a research associate at Birmingham to work on the Project. It was also agreed that, as the DEC20 at Birmingham was used for teaching undergraduate classes, the BLEND user community would be allowed only limited access to the system during term time. The restriction was not easy to impose at the start of the Project because of the limited nature of the DEC20 access control software, and this difficulty led indirectly to one of the early extensions to the system. However, an improved version of the access control software, written at Birmingham, both provided this restriction and guaranteed availability during other periods.

Any computer teleconferencing system supplies facilities for the storage and retrieval of messages by registered users. These facilities are in excess of those provided by electronic mail systems in that the message storage can be organised according to various criteria, such as topic, the group of users having access, and level of confidentiality. Such systems usually retain all messages so that a historical record may be kept of the conference. This can be considered to be similar to the minutes of a committee; and committee and sub-committee structure is probably the best analogy for describing NOTEPAD. It is also possible in any computer teleconferencing system to retrieve messages according to different criteria, for example, messages that the user has not yet read, or perhaps previous messages written by a named user about a particular topic.

Computer teleconferencing systems are usually located in one computer so that would-be users first have to obtain access to that machine before they can use the conferencing facility. This access is usually gained over the public telephone network, although intercomputer networks may also be used. The NOTEPAD system is of this type, and the user community is normally connected to the DEC20 at Birmingham over the dial-up public switched telephone network (PSTN).

Any conferencing software suite is designed to mirror and extend the face-to-face conference or committee meeting onto the computer. In NOTEPAD this mapping is performed in a well-structured and controlled manner. For example a conference may have a small, closed membership such as a committee, or it may be open to everyone as in a general meeting and conversations in the bar. These meetings are called *Activities* in NOTEPAD, and they may have either an 'assigned' or an 'open' membership with the discussion in any one Activity being kept distinct from all others, although messages can be transferred from one Activity to another just as papers can be passed between committees in the face-to-face situation.

Within each Activity the discussion can consist of both public messages (called *Entries* in NOTEPAD terminology) which can be read by all and private messages (*Notes*) between pairs of participants. All text is retained in the Activity so that it can be re-read using a variety of search mechanisms. Past Entries can therefore be regarded as the official record of the Activity and cannot normally be altered, although in later versions of NOTEPAD it was possible for certain designated members to have special editorial purposes.

Because NOTEPAD was originally designed for commercial usage it is also possible to group Activities together into a *Project*. Each Project will have a separate access code registered on the computer and members of one project will not normally know of the existence of any of the others. Moreover if there was an accidental or deliberate break-in to the system, there would be only a very small possibility of reading the Activity files of another Project since all files in the system are encrypted and access can only be gained via NOTEPAD and a second level of password protection. This inbuilt confidentiality extends to Activities within a Project, and the members of the Project are aware only of those closed Activities of which they are named members.

Each Activity has one member, called the *Organiser*, to whom special responsibilities are given. The organiser can inhibit either private or public messages, making the Activity respectively entirely public or read-only, and in the assigned Activities the organiser can add or remove individuals from the membership list. Also the organiser is the only member of the Activity who can close the Activity down, in much the same way as a committee chairman can declare a meeting closed. In fact the roles of Activity organiser and committee chairman are fairly similar. Although the organiser can close the activity down, starting up a new Activity is a task reserved for a separate person, the *Project administrator*, who may or may not be a member of any of the Activities in the Project. The administrator responds to requests from Project members to create new Activities and has the task of ensuring that there is sufficient space in the Project directory for the new Activity. The project administrator also has certain other housekeeping functions such as re-setting the individual password for the more forgetful users.

Within a Project there may be any number of open and assigned Activities, usually each set up around a particular topic or for a special purpose, and the membership lists for these Activities will normally be overlapping. One possible image of the structure of information in NOTEPAD is given in Figure 2.1; this is most nearly the ordinary user's view of the system, whereas the Project administrator' view might be represented by Figure 2.2. These diagrams are not in conflict, but simply emphasise that graphical representations of an abstract structure are a subjective phenomenon.

When users access a Project the directory log-in function ensures that they are immediately connected into the NOTEPAD software suite, and similarly when they decide to end the NOTEPAD session they are automatically logged off the host computer. This procedure serves two quite dissimilar purposes. Firstly it means that users do not need to know anything about the use of the computer except for logging in. The only learning required of new users concerns the use of NOTEPAD itself, in contrast to some current computer conferencing systems which are more closely integrated into the operating system of the host machine and require a greater knowledge on the part of the user. This approach means that NOTEPAD is particularly suitable to the naive or infrequent user. The second result of the log-in function is to ensure that users do not have access to the operating system command level within a Project directory. This serves as a integrity protection mechanism, for although all the Activity files are encrypted and we would not normally expect users to be mischievous, there might be the possibility of accidental damage to some of the files, perhaps resulting from a desire to understand more about the system.

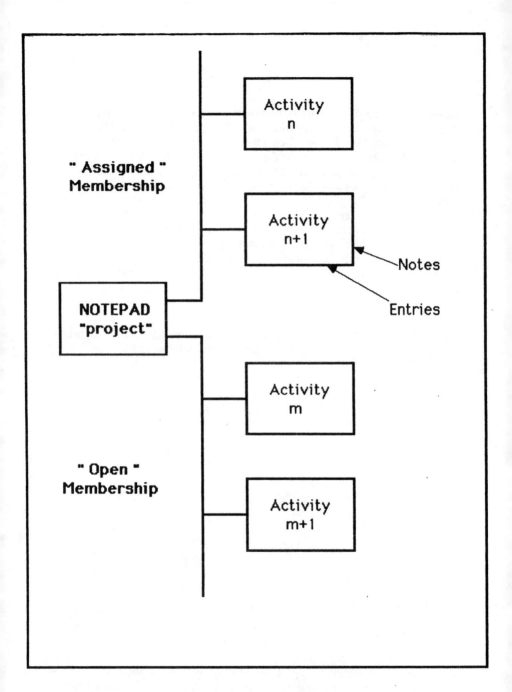

Fig 2.1:   A possible representation of the
NOTEPAD data structure

14

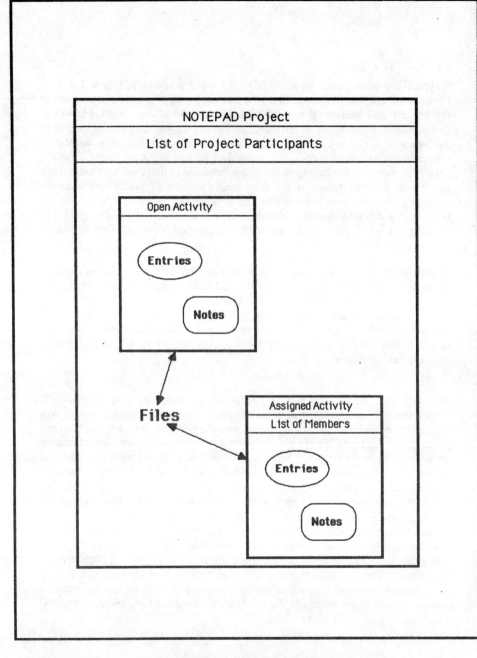

**Fig 2.2: An alternative representation of the
NOTEPAD data structure**

15

A typical log-in sequence for a NOTEPAD Project is shown in Figure 2.3. This illustrates three major points; first, the two levels of password protection - at the Project and individual user levels; second, the ability of NOTEPAD to "recognise" certain types of terminal; and third, the presentation of the list of Activities of which the user is a member. This list of activities is numbered consecutively and there is no indication to the user that any more Activities might exist. The Activity numbering is, therefore, personal to that user, and would only agree with that of another user if they were members of exactly the same set of Activities. It is, therefore, unwise, as some of our users have found out, to refer to Activities by number. However, this restriction only really applies to the assigned Activities, as all Project members are members of all open Activities.

The ability of NOTEPAD to recognise or acknowledge certain makes of terminal (and their look-alikes) is primarily to aid the presentation of data on the display. The primary features used by NOTEPAD for the selected terminals are the 'clear screen' and 'backspace' codes so that NOTEPAD can respectively display new items of data on a fresh screen, thereby avoiding scrolling, and improve the image of edited text, as it is possible for users to edit text while they are preparing new Entries or Notes.

When the user has decided in which Activity to participate, there are a number of *Actions*, or *Commands*, that may be taken. The most frequent Action will normally be reading and writing Notes and Entries but these are not the only possibilities, and NOTEPAD has an interesting approach to the Action control structure. The most common control structures used by software packages are either 'menu-list selection' or 'command-driver'. In the former case, the user is presented with a numbered list of alternatives and is asked to type the number of the required alternative. This is a very simple system to produce and has the added advantage that it is relatively easy to check whether the user has typed in a valid number. However, it has the disadvantage that the menu list must fit onto a single screen, and therefore the menu must either be short or the menu items succinct. This latter point may partially explain the current popularity of menu lists in the form of pictures, or 'ikons', as these may be considered to convey a richness of information in a small physical space. However, for teleconferencing a more serious disadvantage of the menu approach is the time taken, at say 300 baud, to display a complete menu.

```
The University of Birmingham, TOPS-20 Monitor 5(4747)-B05
@LOGIN (USER) BL.BLEND (PASSWORD)
SHARE = 2300  USAGE = 722  TTY = 2/MIN  CPU = 1/SEC  PRIORITY = HIGH
Job 73 on TTY74  11-Mar-85  17:07:51

NOTEPAD is ready
Last Name: DODD
Password:

Good.  Are you using a terminal that prints on paper?
- No

Please type the number corresponding to your make of terminal.
      1  Hazeltine 2000      4  Beehive        7  DEC VT100 (ANSI)
      2  Tektronix 4023      5  Superbee       8  Other
      3  ADM-31              6  DEC VT52

#8

Please enter the number of lines on your CRT terminal
#24
Thank you.
(strike the CR key to continue)

Project:  Alvey News

                          Open Membership

   1   About this Project
   2   General Messages & Discussion
   3   Messages to the Directorate
 * 4   NEWS from Mr.B.W.Oakley (Director)
 * 5     "       "   Mr.S.L.H.Clarke (LDP)
   6     "       "   Mr.D.L.S.Barber (I&C)
   7->   "       "   Mr.C.W.M.Barrow (MMI)
 * 8     "       "   Mr.W.Fawcett (VLSI)
   9     "       "   Mr.D.Talbot (SE)
 * 10    "       "   Dr.D.B.Thomas (IKBS)
 * 11    "       "   Dr.T.E.H.Walker (Admin)
   12  Calendar
```

Fig 2.3: A typical log-in sequence for a NOTEPAD Project

The alternative 'command-driven approach' does not require any information to be sent from the host computer but does require the user to memorise an entire series of commands. Although command words may be well thought out by the system designer they always seem to bear a close resemblance to the command words on another system where, unfortunately, they may have a slightly different meaning. This is especially troublesome to the infrequent user, and the usual recourse is to system 'Help' facilities which gives rise to the same set of problems as the menu-driven approach.

The approach adopted by NOTEPAD is a composite one combining elements of both the command-driven and the menu-driven approaches, and is not unlike the hierarchical menu tree adopted in some systems to overcome the problem of volume of information transmission. NOTEPAD, however, combines a hierarchical command tree structure with an implicit menu at the initial selection level. An implicit menu system contrasts with the more usual (explicit) menu system in that the former does not print out the menu but requires the user to memorise it, or in the case of some NOTEPAD users to label their terminal appropriately. This approach will not work with infrequent users unless the implicit menu contains only the more frequently used commands.

Using this strategy the more frequently used commands, such as selecting the 'write entry' facility, are much shorter than the less frequently used facilities, such as changing your password. This is similar to the variable length coding schemes, e.g. Huffman coding, used in data transmission systems, and produces the lowest level of command traffic overhead. This is particularly advantageous when using a packet switched transmission system, in which the telecommunications costs are primarily dependent on volume of transmission rather than connect time, but also reduces the time the user sends or receives command information.

The complete command tree for a NOTEPAD Activity organiser is shown in Figure 2.4, where the underlined components are those available only to the organiser. The components not underlined are those available to the ordinary members of the Activity. Most of the commands are either self-explanatory, or do not require further elaboration for the purposes of this report. However, one particular command merits further discussion because it opened up the ability to incorporate a number of the enhancements discussed in later chapters.

NOTEPAD ACTION	EXPLANATION	LEVEL 1 PARAMETERS	LEVEL 2 PARAMETERS
1	Write Note	to whom.	
2	Read Note	list of numbers, by, to, between before, after, re "topic".	no text, no heading, first N lines.
3	Select Activity	which	
4	Write Entry		
5	Read Entry	list of numbers, by, before, after, re "topic".	no text, no heading, first N lines.
6	Status of person	All, named person.	
7	Edit	Delete	Note or Entry
		Save (Note or Entry)	in File......
		Submit (File).....	(as Entry or Note to whom)
		Erase	File or Activity
8	Services	Ask (a question)	
		Feedback (the replies)	
		Set	new password
		Set	pagination
		Run	program..........
		Create an Activity	
		Add or Remove	participant
		Inhibit or Restore	Notes or Entries
9	Quit		

Fig 2.4: NOTEPAD Command Hierarchy

This command is the RUN subcommand under the Services Action (Menu item 8) which allows the user to execute one of a number of programs which are external to the NOTEPAD system. The original motivation for this facility was to allow Project groups to incorporate some of their own packages, such as financial modelling suites, into the teleconference system. It is also possible to include the result files from such packages within the Activity record by using the SUBMIT subcommand under the Edit Action (Menu item 7), and even provide an input data file from the Activity record file using the Edit-SAVE subcommand. The RUN subcommand was particularly useful since it allowed us to enhance NOTEPAD in ways to be described in the following chapters.

2.3 Mapping the Electronic Journal onto NOTEPAD

The original purpose of NOTEPAD was to mirror conferences, whereas in BLEND we are concerned with mapping many different forms of interaction from the informal to the formal. However, it is the more formal aspects in which we are specifically interested, and it was these, in the form of the learned journal, which determined the manner in which we used NOTEPAD.

In a computer conference, the public entries are normally fairly short in length, and not necessarily related to each other except in some loose manner. However, a journal article is usually at least a few pages of typescript and, moreover, the reader may wish to read the article in a non-serial manner; for example, reading the abstract and conclusions prior to deciding whether to read the entire article, and even then moving to and fro between the body of the article and the list of references. This suggested that we could not map an article onto a single Entry since NOTEPAD does not provide facilities for moving around within one Entry.

Instead the lead as to which mapping to employ is suggested by Figure 2.3, which shows the list of Activities with which the user is presented on accessing a NOTEPAD Project. This Activity list bears a very close resemblance to the contents list of a journal issue, and it seemed reasonable to use the mapping of each article onto a single Activity. We had already decided to release the journal articles in 'issues' so that we could have regular release dates, and so it was a simple extension to map a journal issue onto a NOTEPAD Project; we would then obtain the 'index' as the list of available open Activities. Figure 2.5 shows the index for one of the journal issues. This figure also illustrates one of the advantages of the electronic journal over its paper equivalent; that of incorporating

```
Project: Computer Human Factors II

                        Open Membership

   1   Editorial   1st May 1983
 * 2   Hartley J & Frase LT   Human and Computer Aids to Writing      [E51.L521]
 * 3   Broadbent et al.  Judgements in Controlling Complex Systems  [E64.L1048]
   4   Shackel et al.    The BLEND-LINC Project after Two Years       [E47.L848]
   5   Sandelin J & Marcus JE  Avoiding a Tower of Babel at Stanford [E52.L755]
 * 6   Review - Hartley & Sloboda on Processing Visible Language 2   [E34.L363]
   7   Discussions/Questions by Readers on 1. Editorial
 * 8   Discussions/Questions by Readers on 2. Hartley & Frase paper
 * 9   Discussions/Questions by Readers on 3. Broadbent et al. paper
  10   Discussion/Questions by Readers on 4. Shackel et al. paper
  11   Discussion/Questions by Readers on 5. Sandelin & Marcus paper
 * 12  Discussion/Questions by Readers on 6. Review by Hartley & Sloboda
```

Fig 2.5: The Contents List for a typical issue of the journal

the discussion on an article within the same issue as the original article. Both would be stored in open Activities, but readers would be prohibited from writing Notes or Entries in the article Activity.

Having decided on the article-to-Activity mapping, we then decided to map each paragraph of the article onto one NOTEPAD Entry, instructing authors to limit their paragraphs to 24 lines of 80 characters maximum, this being the size of a typical VDU screen. A preparatory survey had indicated that this would not be a burdensome restriction as many authors already seemed to limit paragraphs to about this size in conventional journals.

In addition to the advantage of the electronic journal referred to above, Figure 2.5 also illustrates a potential disadvantage - that of not knowing the length of each article. In the hard-copy journal you have immediate knowledge of the length of the article from the number of pages. In the electronic journal there are no such cues, and so we included in the Activity title an indication of the article length in the form of the number of Entries and number of lines.

Editorial convention, in the form of 'Instructions to Authors' (Shackel, 1980) also stipulated that the first three Entries in each article should contain respectively the title and authors, an index to the remainder of the article, and a summary. The index (see Figure 2.6) is especially useful as it lists the Entry numbers for each section of the article and can aid readers in moving around the article. Our initial release of NOTEPAD only allowed access to the Entries/paragraphs by Entry number (either individually or serially through a list of Entry numbers). or by a simple keyword search on the full text of each Entry. However, as an early addition, and at our suggestion, Infomedia provided additional facilities for moving forwards and backwards within the Entry list, and for re- displaying the current Entry in case the reader wished to take a printed copy.

This was as far as we were able to progress within the NOTEPAD structure, but we were still short of our aim of providing good reading aids, and had not yet addressed the problem of providing aids for the journal refereeing and editorial processes. The following chapters will describe how these were incorporated.

So far we have only described the mapping of the electronic journal, but as stated in Chapter 1 we were also interested in other types of communication. The

```
[2]  Hartley (and-Frase)     1-May-83  11:42 PM


(2)  Contents                                          Entry Nos.
==============                                          =========
    (3) Summary                                         3
    (4) Introduction                                    4-5
    (5) Human aids to writing                           6-7
    (6) The classification with examples                8-22
    (7) Figure 1                                        23-24
    (8) Computer aids to writing                        25
    (9) Figure 2                                        26-28
   (10) Output from the computer programs               29-40
   (11) Discussion                                      41-48
   (12) References                                      49
   (13) Acknowledgements                                50
   (14) Authors' addresses                              51
```

Fig 2.6: The Contents List for an article in the journal

mapping for these was primarily defined by that for the refereed journal, so that for example we mapped the poster papers journals onto one Project with each article and its associated discussion forming one Activity. Most of the remaining communication types could be mapped directly onto computer conferencing, and we chose to have a single Project (NEWS) to accommodate these (see fig.2.7). Finally we set aside a Project (AUTHOR) in which each community member could have a personal Activity as writing space, and a restricted membership Project for the editorial and refereeing procedures.

Project: News from 1st May 1983

Open Membership

1 Messages
* 2 LINC members & Who's who
3 LINC Projects and Activities
4 Advice & Query Corner
5 LINC News
* 6 Computer Human Factors Qs & As
7 Teleconference on Mail and Conference System Needs
8 Chit-Chat
9 Jim Hartley's Questionnaire
10 Teleconference - Electronic Journals
11 Teaching Matters
* 12 Teleconference - 1985 LINC P & A Structure

Assigned Membership

13 BLEND Co-ordination
14 Project Co-ordination
* 15 Discussions on new versions of Notepad
16 Discussions on possible new communities on BLEND
17 TORCH users' group

**Fig 2.7: The Activity list for the NOTEPAD Project containing
the less formal communication modes**

3. THE NEED FOR SOFTWARE ENHANCEMENTS

Although NOTEPAD allowed several levels of communication, it was found necessary to enhance the facilities to aid users in their tasks, for example authors in editing and sending manuscripts to the host computer, or readers in skipping round a journal paper, and to make the interaction more simple and consistent. This chapter describes the process, rationale and extent of these enhancements, and the following chapter describes in more detail some additional items of software that have been written to extend the basic facilities offered by NOTEPAD. Although the changes made are modest (by the standards feasible in computer systems designs), they have made a considerable difference to the ease of use and amount of use.

3.1 Development Procedure

Although it was generally agreed that NOTEPAD was the most 'user-friendly' software suite available for computer teleconferencing, it was to be put to use for rather different purposes.

The initial development of the system was a direct consequence of analysis and discussions by interested parties. Thus it rested on the 'expert' opinion of those experienced in computer teleconferencing and in editorial procedure. The first enhancements were also developed by way of the 'expert' opinion of members of the BLEND team in conjunction with initial periods of trial usage.

Before the main usage of NOTEPAD in the experimental programme of electronic journals, a period of 3 months was allowed for trials by all users who had the necessary equipment. The users were computer specialists or human factors specialists (psychologists and ergonomists) who were active in the field of Computer Human Factors (see Shackel, 1982). Their initial reaction to the BLEND system as naive users was qualified by expertise in this field. Thus the expert opinion of the Project team and the 'expert' users' reactions contributed to the first set of enhancements which were partially implemented in the version of the software made available for the start of the main experimental programme.

During the course of main usage, developments and reviews continued. Necessarily, in a system with expanding facilities whose usage was hypothesised rather than actual, expert opinion continued to play a part. However, evidence for different enhancements came from many other more formal sources, such as:

- observations by a researcher of first-time use to see what expectations the users had and what problems were encountered

- analysis of HELP requests by phone, answerphone and as messages in the BLEND system

- formal controlled experiments on certain aspects, including part of the dialogue, structuring of papers and aids to reading on-line

- analysis of usage data collected by the software.

More generalised formal experiments were planned for Year 3 (1983) of the experimental programme, to assess fully the facilities needed by a software suite to support electronic journals. This process for the evolutionary design and enhancement of a system is similar to that recommended in Eason, 1982.

3.2 Areas requiring enhancement

The initial development and subsequent research quickly illustrated four major areas in which difficulty was experienced:-

1. The wish to accomplish multiple tasks while logged into the computer.

2. 'Knowing where one is' in the database structure.

3. Consistency in concept and command structure.

4. Handling large pieces of text.

Each will be discussed with examples where applicable.

1. The wish to accomplish multiple tasks when logged into the computer.

The structure of NOTEPAD is so designed that each commercial organisation or group using the system would have a separate secure area, with a password. The BLEND Project Director initiated, after discussion, a structure which placed different types of work Activity in different areas, for example writing papers in one, reading journals in another, exchanging news in yet another. Almost at once it was discovered that while some users did separate out these different functions operationally, others would log in and wish to be able to pass easily and quickly from one area to another. Consequently an additional level was introduced (see Figure 3.1), and to establish whether this level was in fact necessary a data collection package was introduced.

Questions may be asked such as 'In general, do users log in to accomplish one thing, for example referee a paper or read a journal?' or 'Do users go to a terminal and then accomplish everything relating to the BLEND system in one session?' Answers depend on many factors including working style, work situation and access to terminal equipment, but preliminary inspection shows that while some users only log into one Project in one on-line session, others log into many. Thus a facility to move between Projects is both needed and useful, provided that it does not interfere with use by those not requiring it.

Introducing another level, however, brings other problems such as 'knowing where one is' and 'knowing what there is to see'

2. 'Knowing where one is'

Knowing where one is and where to go in a two-level hierarchical tree structure may seem a trivial problem. However, one experiment on Viewdata illustrated the difficulties of searching with goal acquisition in just two levels which caused much distress to the subjects (Van Nes and Van der Heijden, 1980). It does seem, though, that a two-level system appears to be the best for moderate sized hierarchical systems, both from a small user survey (Cole, 1981) which showed that this is the preferred number for many office filing systems, and from an experiment on menu-based on-line search (Miller, 1981). The number of Activities and Projects in BLEND form a hierarchical system of comparable size to those investigated in the studies, which indicate that breadth is preferred over depth for an increase in the number of items.

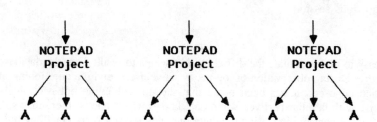

Original: each Project is password protected

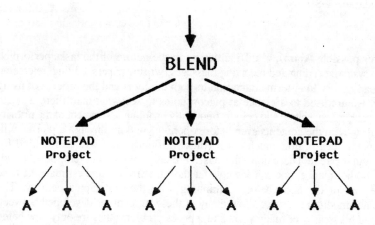

Final: only BLEND and a few special Projects are
password protected

Fig 3.1: Development of the Structure of BLEND

The problems of databases in information systems are confounded in BLEND by the addition of new text in many places, raising the questions 'Where does the user find it?' and 'How does the user keep up to date?' The interactive nature of computer teleconferencing that allows users to write in many places also leads to the difficulty of remembering where some message was written or received in a previous session.

It is easy to underestimate the difficulty that seems to result from the database structure. During observation of log-ins by naive users, and the questioning of experienced users, it has been noted that the difficulties do not necessarily diminish with familiarity. Even when one 'knows where one is', there may still be difficulty incurred in getting to where one then wishes to go. Handling both the conceptual structure of the database and the commands necessary have proved awkward for some users, and several alternative user aids and forms of support have been necessary (as are frequently recommended but rarely supplied, cf. Damodaran, 1981).

Further possible 'knowing' difficulties lie in the nature of the tasks performed on the system: sending and receiving messages, writing papers, editing, refereeing and reading. By long-term adaptation to both the tools and the process of using paper, we are used to a glance at pigeon-holes to see what mail there is, with the envelope size, shape, and colour, frequently enabling assessment of the priority of dealing with the contents even before opening. A skim through a journal will give us the idea of how much effort (time, difficulty etc.) will be required for a particular paper. These and other tasks are easy to interrupt temporarily and, with another glance, one can see how far they are through and estimate the time to the end of the task, before continuing with the interrupted activity. The computer medium does not allow many of these procedures developed between man and his tools over many years and it poses problems that are only now being considered.

Electronic mail has treated some of these problems by having a mailbox presented to the user with informative envelopes when he or she logs in (see for example discussion in Uhlig, 1981). The user may then place the messages in a personal categorisation and database (including a waste-bin if desired!). Several substantial attempts have been made to improve the locational sense of databases that many people build into their office system with the aim of knowing what there is, and where and how to travel to it (Bolt, 1979; Spence & Apperley, 1982).

Computer teleconferencing, with its concept of an ongoing discussion with conference entries gradually accumulating over many hours or several years, has a rather different structure from electronic mail and presents difficulties for users with many conferences. Some computer conferencing suites, e.g. COM, (Palme & Enderin, 1982) have a flexible order of conferences with those containing new messages being placed at the top. Some users, however, complain about the directiveness of the system and of never quite knowing where they are.

To summarise: there can be difficulties for the user in

1. knowing where one is

2. knowing where and how one can go

3. knowing what there is new to see

4. knowing what what-there-is-to-see involves

5. knowing whether one has seen everything

6. knowing where one saw something previously.

In the BLEND system there have been a few enhancements to obviate some of these difficulties, though this is only a beginning in tackling the problems experienced. Far more radical innovations are needed for the future.

In 'knowing where one is', four principles have been used:

1. reinforcing redundancy

2. help when requested

3. returning to a known point and starting again

4. operating from one conceptual position.

31

For an example of the principle of reinforcing redundancy consider the many different cues that are used for any set of objects. For example, journals in a pile may be remembered in several ways, such as colour ('the red one'), distinguishing marks ('the one with a coffee stain'), size ('the big one') etc. These are reinforced by each search in the process of doing other tasks.

With computer text messages this principle is applied by giving short redundant information to remind the user, possibly subconsciously, where he or she is. The Project title is added above each Activity title to form a pair whenever each is displayed and a page-header facility has been introduced to set a running header (for printer or VDU). A further proposal (not able to be implemented) was for the title of the Activity just left to be displayed in order to orientate movements around each Project.

Most important for the user is probably the facility to ask 'Where am I?'. Pressing three keys (two of them the Return, or Enter, key) sends a

statement "You are in Project ... Activity ..."

Casual observation of computers in use shows that many people, whether occasional or long-standing users, have a 'let's start again' fallback position which they find helpful. Hence it is useful to have a facility to jump out of what one is doing to a known point and start again.

Accordingly commands have been implemented and made consistent to enable the user to return to such start points. Subsequently, annotated printouts of some individuals' use clearly indicate that they made use of such a strategy.

3.   Consistency in concept and command structure

Watching a young person using the telephone for the first few times can be highly instructive. Most of us are so familiar with the process that we forget that it is a learnt one, that the protocol is different, that we speak differently as is necessary without non-verbal cues and that the medium affects the content of the message. For example, one has to give a verbal cue to indicate that one has finished speaking and that the other person has an opportunity. In normal conversation this is non-verbal.

The difference in the conceptual framework of the child as a naive user of the telephone and that of the experienced user is analogous to the difference found between naive users of computer systems and the experts. There is, however, an important distinction. In the child's case, there is clearly no alternative solution to the mismatch of conceptual frameworks other than that of learning and adopting the widespread convention, whereas in the computer system there are often alternatives available.

One such example occurred in the BLEND system, as a result of users' misconception concerning the operating system of the host computer. Commands to the computer are usually ended by pressing the Return, or Enter, key, and before users end the command, they may invoke help facilities and use control characters for editing purposes, these being thought of as a separate category of communication with the computer. The DEC2060 has a help facility obtained by pressing just the question mark '?', which is treated as such a character, i.e. not as a command, and therefore does not require the terminating Return character.

The conceptual framework for naive users of NOTEPAD might be stated as 'End all commands by pressing Return key, except when using control characters'. Unfortunately a number of users thought that the '?' character was a command rather than a control character, and acted accordingly. This second framework came into direct conflict in the system so that users responding with a question mark and return (? <CR>) in one particular place were logged out of the computer. The conflict was resolved by allowing *both* frameworks to be acceptable, despite the difficulty expressed by the system designers. The user could type a question mark followed immediately by a Return or not as chosen; after a delay however, if a Return was typed then it was taken in read-ahead mode of the host computer to be the next command. In this way the conceptual framework of both sets of users could be maintained.

It is thus important for systems designers to know what type of conceptual framework the users are likely to bring to their interactions. Gringas, 1976, has shown that computer systems analysts have psychological self-images that are very similar to their image of an ideal user of the system, which can lead to a poor fit with actual users.

There have been several attempts to classify users according to the particular needs of each group (for example see Eason, Damodaran & Stewart, 1974; Gaines, 1981; Maguire, 1982). The closest classification to describe the present users of BLEND might be 'casual', i.e. those who only use the system occasionally. Cuff, 1980, has discussed the dialogue requirements and other needs for such users. However, he particularly emphasises casual users who are naive, and the problems of those who are otherwise (e.g. those who are computer 'experts' for other systems) are not addressed.

The first community to use BLEND was a collection of human factors and computer academics (Loughborough Information Network Community - LINC) and in experience they ranged from the most naive to the most experienced in the use of computer systems. However, only logging into the system between twice a week and once a fortnight brings some problems irrespective of computer experience.

The naive users bring no understanding with them to the system and take the best rational rule available to explain the system's behaviour, which will often be confounded (as in the example above about what it is that constitutes a command). Experienced users frequently have substantial preconceived ideas and have already learned many command structures. To learn a new structure not often used (relative to other systems) would in any case impose a high memory load, but they have to cope with the frustration that they know exactly what they want to do with the system conceptually but do not know which commands to give to accomplish it (see Figure 3.2).

Thus for this kind of 'occasional' user it is suggested that features such as high consistency in the command structure with ease of use should take priority over a wide range of available commands at each point. The need for conceptual consistency throughout all related areas of the system should take priority even sometimes at the cost of an individual facility.

4.   Handling large pieces of text

In the past, large pieces of text in a computer have usually been treated in a single lump. When the text is presented for reading or editing, the computer scrolls through until the appropriate point is reached. Whereas there are many situations where this is appropriate, it is not so when editing on-line at 300 baud (a full-length paper of 6,000 words takes about 20 minutes to be transmitted down

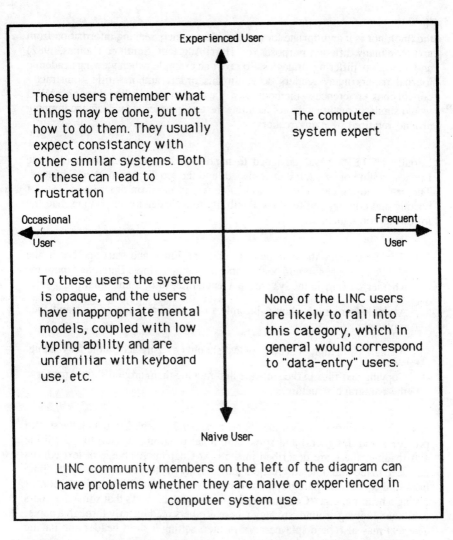

Fig 3.2: Location of LINC Community members with
regard to experience and use of BLEND

the line), nor is it appropriate for reading. Researchers seeking information from text have many different purposes (cf. Harri-Augstein, Smith & Thomas, 1982) and thus adopt differing strategies. To give one example, when viewing academic journal papers many readers do so in this order: author - title - abstract - conclusions - references - methodology. Viewing papers on-line through a VDU would similarly require a way of handling the text in order to facilitate the jumping around required by many readers.

Initially NOTEPAD was designed to handle messages which, as conference Entries, could not be altered or replaced, and then to display them in sequence. The new requirement to be able to handle text in the form described above for writing and editing, and to allow flexibility to a reader for displaying, had the following consequences:

- For consistency the command to end one Entry and start another in the middle of a paper should be the same as ending a single Entry, and the same whether writing on the system, in a text editor, or by some other procedure.

- A single paragraph should be able to be accessed for editing and then replaced.

- A single paragraph or section of text should be easily accessible for reading.

- Copying text-files in the software and moving them around should preserve the paragraph structure.

A suitable structure was developed (after considerable negotiation with the system providers and designers) and some additional programs written to aid editing and reading; these are described in the next Chapter. A choice of text editors has been made available and readers may display the text on a VDU by stepping back and forward in paragraph-sized chunks, by giving the 'page' number, or giving a heading, e.g. "Conclusions". The usage data shows that some members exhibit a 'jumping around' strategy whereas others read linearly through a paper. The text may also be displayed on a printer, setting a short header and having pages automatically numbered.

The relationship between this kind of software, to support reading for skimming and scanning, and the structure of the paper itself is the subject of on-going research since there is a priori no reason for only permitting linear structure for text of journal paper length.

The problems identified above in knowing where one is and knowing what the task involves apply also to the situation of individual papers being read on a VDU screen. It is possible that technology may evolve so that cues will be available which will be equivalent to seeing the scope of the contents. However, at the present time the problem is similar to viewing a paper through a small window. Suggested solutions for this have varied from a visual emulation of a pair of pages open with indication of relation to the other pages (Benest & Jones, 1982) to a full tree-structure access.

3.3 Discussion

This chapter has discussed some of the problems encountered when using a software suite developed for computer teleconferencing for a greater range of purposes, including electronic journals and many other levels of scientific communication. The solutions presented are appropriate to this particular application but there are general lessons to be learnt from both the procedure and the content.

In the development of such systems a limit on financial resources or time is almost certain, and the dialogue between human factors experts and systems experts may appear to require additional time. The attitudes of both can be heavily confounded by the knowledge that, given sufficient time and resources, a 'really magnificent' system could be achievable! However, the need to allocate sufficient time for this dialogue is crucial.

Although the enhancements presented here are modest by any standards, they have made the system much more acceptable to the users. This can be attributed to the procedure adopted of involvement with the users at different levels, and the coherent presentation of research and documentary evidence of the need for change to the systems designers. Indeed, the systems designers challenged the need for most of the enhancements at the start, but later admitted that they themselves had found these enhancements useful.

One particular area of note is that the co-operation between system designers and computer human factors engineers in the BLEND experimental programme has resulted in an acceptance of different frameworks of thought which have equal validity. The alteration of the software to accommodate two differing command structures is a radical change from the usual opinion that only one such should be provided and the users should learn it.

4. READING, REFEREEING AND BROWSING IN BLEND

Throughout the study we have viewed BLEND as a testbed electronic journal system, and the software has been enhanced at a number of points in the programme. The earlier enhancements have been described in Chapter 3 and, except for the facility to move easily between projects, these were carried out at our request by Infomedia who alone had access to the source code. However, these were not the only enhancements to the software that have been included during the period of the experimental programme, and this chapter describes three of the more useful enhancements.

Reading papers on-line poses particular problems because of the limited amount of material available to view on a typical cathode ray tube, which hinders the use of normal visual cues such as layout and easily distinguishable headings. Refereeing papers on-line poses problems in that it is difficult to make comments and marks on the script itself, for example in the margins next to the relevant piece of text. Browsing through references and abstracts also has the problem of lack of visual cues. Experimental utility software has been developed to handle some of these problems and is being used in BLEND for reading and refereeing papers and in the *References, Abstracts and Annotations Journal*, in which readers may have annotations appended to the authors' abstracts.

The approach adopted for these later enhancements has been to make use of the ability to include inferior processes within NOTEPAD using the RUN subcommand referred to in Section 2.2. This facility allowed us to include self-contained code modules with the general NOTEPAD command structure without having access to the source code of NOTEPAD. This has proved to be an extremely valuable feature and, probably, of itself justified our choice of NOTEPAD, though this advantage only became evident with hindsight.

Since we were uncertain of the exact functional specifications of the reading, refereeing and browsing software we used a method of development based on a series of evolving prototypes.

Prototyping as a means of validating functional requirements and specifying software has been described elsewhere, (Dodd 1980; Gomaa & Scott 1981; Dearnley & Mayhew, 1983). The prototype software was written in the locally-available text processing language ATOL (Axford and others 1979; Dodd and others, 1982) and the production process for the current application is described in Maude & Dodd, 1985.

Accessing Papers On-Line

The problem of reading papers on-line is akin to that of reading a copy of a newspaper through a 4ins x 2ins hole. The normal visual cues of layout and an overall view are gone. This problem occurs whether reading a paper, refereeing a paper for an academic journal, or browsing in the hope of finding something interesting.

Many computer systems have a command to display a text file on the user's terminal. It appears as a continuous scroll, possibly stopping at fixed length intervals until the user decides to continue. When working from a distance using a public network there is a restriction on the speed of transmission, typically 30 or 120 characters per second. Reading papers in this linear fashion at these relatively slow speeds is probably not the way that many people would choose given an available 'hard-copy' alternative.

During a survey of scientists due to use the BLEND system, those interviewed were asked how they approached a journal in order to read papers (Pullinger, 1983b). Three strategies or purposes seemed to be adopted:

1. The general pattern of filtering through the stages - title: abstract: results/conclusions: references: full text: possible photocopy.

2. A preliminary filter of title and abstract followed by a request for a photocopy for later reading.

3. Skimming through articles for new ideas without particular note of paper content.

These strategies are not compatible with linear display of text or with the relatively slow speeds available.

Initial Facilities in BLEND

In the Computer Human Factors Journal the layout of papers is standardised (Shackel, 1983), and Entries are numbered consecutively, the first three being the title and author, contents and summary respectively. Thus Entry number two is always the contents and refers to the other sections by Entry number. In NOTEPAD the facilities for reading are designed for reviewing past entries in a conferencing situation, and are more appropriate for finding something that one remembers having read than for reading something new. (New Entries appear on the screen automatically on NOTEPAD unless there are more than six, in which case the user has a choice of where to start). The process of reading a paper would consist of selecting a list of Entries which are then displayed in the order given. The options for choosing Entries for the list include giving Entry numbers directly and searching for occurrences of a given string.

4.1 BLEND Software for Reading Papers

As described in Chapter 3 the first new facility introduced into the BLEND system to aid reading of papers was built into the NOTEPAD software by Infomedia Corporation at the request of the BLEND Project team. On setting up the list of Entries to be read, the user can also specify if he or she wishes to use a 'step' function. This allows him or her to step backwards and forwards through the paper. After each Entry is displayed, the user has the option of going on to the next Entry, back to the previous one, repeating the one already displayed (used, for instance if, on reading the Entry, it is clear that a printed copy would be useful) or aborting the reading session. The main differences between this and the most usual methods are that:

1. It is possible to move backwards.

2. It is possible to stop the reading process in the middle of a list of Entries or a paper.

3. The text is displayed Entry by Entry instead of stopping when the screen gets full.

4. For recognised terminals, the screen is cleared and the text displayed from the top. This means that the user reads still text, not continuously moving text.

Although the step function provides these additional facilities a separate utility program was written to enable the users to adopt further their chosen reading strategy for hard copy papers. In addition to replicating the facilities provided in the NOTEPAD step function, an additional command to select any Entry by giving its Entry number was implemented. Thus the user can have random access to the whole paper. The command to go back to the previous Entry has the meaning 'go back to the Entry most recently displayed'; further use of this subcommand displays the Entry accessed before that one and so on until the original first Entry is redisplayed. Also a string search command was introduced to scan the first lines of the Entries, making it possible to go straight to 'conclusions', for example. Three additional facilities were therefore added:

5. The facility to jump around the text.

6. A command to return to the previously displayed section of text.

7. A string search on first lines of Entries to enable jumping to named section headings.

Incorporating these new features into the utility program allows readers to use reading strategies approaching their normal ones. For those who go through the paper in a specified order, the Entries may be called up by use of the string search command. The search examines the text on the first two lines of each Entry thus avoiding finding references to the title in other parts of the text. If the section titles are not standard, for example when there is no 'conclusions' or 'discussion' section, the reader always has the option of displaying the contents of Entry 2 first and then going to the appropriate section.

The facility to go back to the entry previously displayed may be used when looking at another part of the text and then returning; for example, when checking a reference, diagram or figure and then returning to the text from where it was referenced. This might be considered the electronic equivalent of keeping your finger in the page. A summary of the commands provided is shown in Figure 4.1.

```
Abort                  - End running of program
Forward, <return>      - Display next Entry
Back, Previous         - Display Entry most recently
                           seen
Repeat                 - Diplay current Entry again
<number of Entry>      - Display the Entry of that
                           number
"<string>"             - Display the next Entry with
                           a title containing the string
"                      - Repeat the last string
                           request
```

Fig 4.1: Commands in the Reading aid program

4.2 BLEND Software for Refereeing Papers

When a paper is refereed, comments are written about the paper in a report to the journal editor. The act of refereeing is not just reading the paper and writing a report; some referees like to write on the script itself, making notes and marks in the margins. If these notes are to be passed on to the editor, it is important that they are referenced to the relevant line or paragraph. In an electronic journal the script may not be supplied as hard copy and so this process is not a trivial one.

Software has been developed in the BLEND system to allow the referees to make comments and 'marks' attached to Entries in the script, thus going some way towards replicating the activity described above. Every Entry in the paper may have a comment tied to it which is available to be read on request, so that the referee may make a series of comments which are then tied to the relevant Entries, while to maintain confidentiality, the comments and paper are made available only to the referee.

The software permits access to the comment independently of the Entries, and the referee can give commands to step through the comments one by one, to display all the comments, or to see individual ones, as well to remove, replace and create them.

Another thing that referees sometimes wish to do is to make a mark in the margin in order that the section can easily be picked out again; this facility has also been included in the software. One command marks the current Entry so that each time the Entry is displayed there is also a short note at the bottom 'Entry Marked'. Many Entries may have marks and these can be displayed all together or one at a time quite independently of the rest.

One way in which this structure of the text and marks may be represented is shown in Figure 4.2.

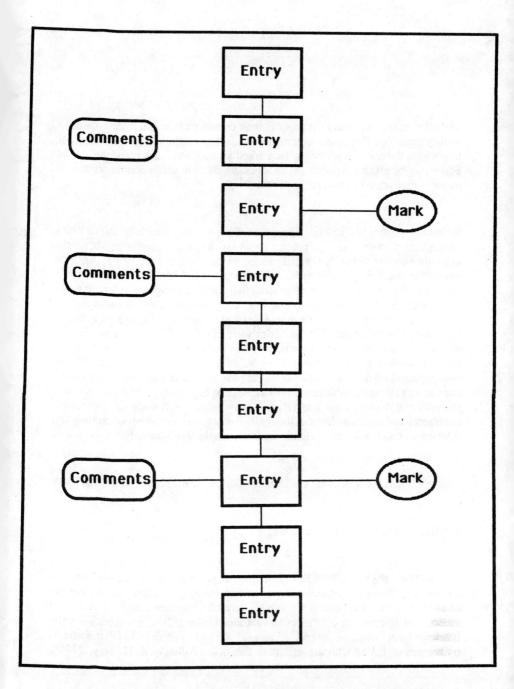

Fig 4.2: An example of the Entry, comment and mark structure in the Referee program

The referees may now read the paper in their chosen manner and make comments as they go along. Particular sections to which they might wish to refer later, or might wish the editor to refer, may be marked for easy access later, and the journal editor may be given a synopsis of, or access to, these in-script comments as well as any other report conveyed in private.

It should be noted that this only goes part of the way in mimicking the facilities available to the referee using a printed version of the paper. Comments and marks are only specific to the Entry and cannot be attached to a particular word or phrase for instance. Thus it may be difficult to underline spelling mistakes, circle a part of a figure, etc. On the other hand there are advantages in refereeing on-line which are not available to the hard-copy referee. One of these is that communication with the editor can be faster and more of a dialogue than a report. Questions may be asked as if the script were in front of both of them. Such a dialogue, in a conferencing system, may be synchronous (i.e. both referee and editor present at the same time) or asynchronous (i.e. the dialogue extending over a period of time with only one using the system at any one time). More unusual refereeing possibilities also exist, such as multi-way discussions between the editor and more than one referee, again with a soft copy of the script, comments and marks in front of them all. Possibilities also exist for putting the referees in touch with the original authors, maybe anonymously.

Figure 4.3 lists the additional commands available to the referee in this Activity

4.3 BLEND Software for Browsing

On 1st May, 1983, the BLEND experimental programme started the on-line *References, Abstracts and Annotations Journal* (RAAJ). This contains a database of bibliographic references in the subject area of Computer Human Factors up to 1981 and more recent references and authors' abstracts from selected journals. It is hoped that evaluative (or critical) annotations will be appended to the abstracts by readers of RAAJ who are expert in the field (Pullinger & Howey, 1984).

The implications that have been drawn from previous studies and the surveys conducted by the HUSAT Research Centre have led to the following requirements:

```
Comment            - Make a comment on current Entry
See                - Display the comment tied to
                       current Entry
Delete Comment     - Delete the comment tied to
                       current Entry
Overwrite          - Replace the comment tied to
                       current Entry
Last Comment       - Display last Comment
Next Comment       - Display next Comment
                     ( these two commands allow the
                       referee to browse through the
                       comments.)
Every Comment      - Lists all the comments
Mark               - Mark the current Entry
Delete Mark        - Remove mark on current Entry
Last Mark          - Display last Entry marked
Next Mark          - Display next Entry marked
                     ( these two comments allow the
                       referee to browse through the
                       marked Entries.)
Every Mark         - Lists all marked Entries
```

Fig 4.3: Additional Commands in the Refereeing aid program

1. a separation of the database into current journals and a large collection of earlier information

2. a flexible software aid for browsing and searching, though not a sophisticated search tool

3. the possibility of annotating references to guide others as to their content and value

The RAAJ provides two types of information, factual (references and abstracts or summaries) and evaluative (annotations). An annotation is an evaluative or critical comment or 'note' intended to be written by BLEND users and appended to the reference and abstract. Annotations are intended to provide a value judgement or summary of the contents of the original documents for the benefit of other journal readers.

It was recognised that the software needed for browsing the RAAJ would need to be similar to that for refereeing in that comments (annotations) must be attached to the Entry concerned. Facilities for moving about the abstracts would also be similar, but some features needed to be changed.

The most fundamental change to the software was that of searching. When reading and refereeing a paper it is important to be able to find headings and titles and so the first two lines are searched when a string search command is performed, whereas in an abstracts journal it is important to be able to search for keywords, authors, dates etc. The database was, therefore, set up with keywords on special lines which are indicated by an asterisk. Each of these lines also includes the Entry number. When a keyword search is carried out, all the keyword lines containing that keyword are displayed and the users may then choose the particular Entry by number. This and the other reading commands may be used to browse through the database.

Comments may be seen, as in the referee utility, and also browsed by use of the next comment and last comment commands. Additionally it was considered important to be able to browse through comments by certain people whose judgement is highly respected by the browser, thus filtering on some of the annotations, and so string searches may also be performed on comments. A major difference between this software and the refereeing utility is that the comments are not confidential but are available to all readers, and if a reader wishes to make an annotation it is sent as a private note to the sub-editor and then placed in the database in the appropriate format.

Marking references is another useful facility as this may be used to make a note of important references found while the user browses so that a copy may be taken later. Thus before the browsing session is finished, the marked abstracts (possibly together with their associated annotations) may be printed out, reviewed or stored in the user's microcomputer. As RAAJ is available to all users, all marks have to be associated with a particular individual to avoid confusion, and only exist for one session.

One of the objectives of the BLEND programme is an evaluation of the usage of the software and consequently a monitor has been built into all the software mentioned in order to log the actions taken by individuals. The monitor records what commands are made, which Entries are read and in what order and the starting and finishing time, though to maintain confidentiality the referees' comments are not recorded in the log. With the data recorded it will be possible to do an analysis of users' on-line reading habits as well as of the usage of the various commands provided.

4.4 Discussion

The changes made from the original NOTEPAD software for reading may seem quite small. However, we believe that these changes make a much more usable system allowing the readers to read papers in a style to which they are more accustomed.

The usage log will provide more information as to the reading habits of BLEND users. The analysis of this data will take place at a later date and the results will be published in one of the other reports; however, during an initial trial experiment (Hills, Hull & Pullinger, 1983) it was noted that some people are quite prepared to read journal articles on-line in a linear fashion.

The philosophy behind the design of these software utilities has been to provide users with software tools which enable them to take actions similar to those taken when dealing with hard-copy articles. Thus readers can skip around a paper in any order they wish, referees can make comments and marks in the 'margin' and browsers going through a set of references, abstracts and annotations can mark those required for future reference. In this way the growing communities of users of the BLEND system can more easily comprehend the facilities that are being made available to them.

One can conceive many other possibilities such as direct referencing to other papers available on the system (e.g. on seeing a reference the user could immediately get a copy of that paper); voice-over comments allowing referees to express their opinions verbally, the comments being tied to the particular place in the text; diagrams that move; automated sorting of a paper into the individual user's preferred order of reading, e.g. title, abstract, conclusions etc. Such facilities are too varied to be provided as a matter of course in an experimental system. When dealing with a voluntary and busy community it is important that there should be only a small learning overhead before the system can be used, and therefore the facilities should adopt a not too unusual approach. Any other features would need further evaluative research to establish their acceptability and potential and so work is being done in parallel on some of these.

It has not been easy to make changes to the NOTEPAD suite without having the source code, and five procedures have been used:

1. running NOTEPAD as an inferior process to another program.

2. running NOTEPAD as a superior process to another program.

3. replacing separately supplied modules of NOTEPAD.

4. accessing files produced by NOTEPAD.

5. requesting changes from the writers of the software.

These produce a 'shell' round the NOTEPAD software, so that the user is protected from escape into the mainframe operating system, and also provide a consistent viewpoint for accomplishing the tasks required.

The problems for casual users inherent in such a system are easily underestimated. The BLEND research team now know that a complete restructuring of software is required for electronic journals with messaging and conferencing facilities, but that this should be done in conjunction with a group of users who maintain a regular but casual use (cf Eason, 1982).

5. EVALUATION OF THE ADDITIONAL SOFTWARE PROGRAMS

5.1 Evaluation of the Software

Having introduced new software programs, it was then considered necessary to decide whether the time and resources spent on the development had been worthwhile. At a general level this seemed to be true from the reactions of LINC members in a telephone survey carried out in November 1983 (see BLEND Report No. 1). In this survey many users reported that the software had been improved and enhanced, some voluntarily saying that it was more 'user-friendly'! Nevertheless, there are many aspects of the system for which suggested improvements are still to be made.

The evaluation considered the two major contributions to user software written at the University of Birmingham, the program to change from Project to Project, and the suite of programs based on the one developed to allow flexible reading of articles, with the aim of deciding whether these were useful, and whether experience with them suggested further modifications.

There is one further category of software programs written at the University of Birmingham. This comprises those utility programs for processing or administrative functions which were found essential in order to accomplish a particular task. An example of this is a program to remove double spacing blank lines from a file being sent from a Wordstar terminal that itself does not have the proper communications protocol to handle this aspect. A brief description of these programs is given in Section 5.4. However, the evaluation of these lies solely in the fact that without them the tasks of operation would have been severely constrained or impossible.

5.2 Evaluation of the Program to change Projects

The reasons for, and development of, this program have already been described in the previous chapters. Here we note the reasons why it was thought useful and what further modifications were suggested.

5.2.1 Usefulness of the Program

The structure of the BLEND system and the introduction of this program meant that all people accessing the system were forced to use it. This means that evaluation does not reflect the voluntary use made of this one particular program among other possibilities or tasks but only whether it was used for the purpose for which it was designed, i.e. did users change projects within a session?

There are three pieces of evidence that suggest that it was indeed used in that way. First, examples from the data recorded by the computer on the sequence of Projects and Activities indicate that many people go into several Projects sequentially. This would have been a difficult task without the program. Examples of the use made of the program are given in Figure 5.1.

An overview of the entry into different Projects over time shows a similar picture. The length of sessions that people spend on the BLEND system forms an exponentially decaying distribution of times. This can be most clearly seen in Figure 5.2 in the Project NEWS. Most accesses are made to NEWS and the majority of time is spent in this one Project. Observation of examples of access behaviours, e.g. Figure 5.1, show themselves here both by the generally flatter shape of the distributions for other Projects, and by the bumps that appear. The former indicates that accesses are normally made to NEWS and then use is made of the program to change Projects. The bumps confirm that there must generally be cases where this is true, particularly showing in some of the CHF (*Computer Human Factors*) journals, the SR (*Software Reviews*) Journal, the *Poster Papers Journal* and RAAJ (*The References, Abstracts and Annotations Journal*).

One other piece of evidence for the usefulness of the new software can be found in the complaints that occurred during the short periods when it is not available for access to a new Project. One example was found when the *Alvey Newsletter* was placed on-line. Access to this was permitted to the group of readers of the published and printed newsletter if they requested it. The design of the system meant that a group of users had direct access into, and only into, the newsletter on the BLEND system. However it was found that some LINC members who already used the BLEND system wanted to include the newsletter amongst the normal set of Projects. LINC members were unwilling to consider any alternative but to have access incorporated into the program to change Projects so that they could first access NEWS and then the *Alvey Newsletter*.

Example 1

Project	Activity
News	Messages
Referee	Paper
News	Messages

Example 3

Project	Activity
News	Messages
"	Q&A corner
"	LINC News
"	Conference
Author	Advice & Help
"	Editorial-messages
SR	Editorial
News	Conference
CC1-2	Paper

Example 2

Project	Activity
News	Messages
Poster	Editorial-messages
News	Messages
"	Q&A corner
"	LINC News
"	Chit-Chat
Poster	Index
"	Paper
"	Paper
"	Paper
"	Paper

Example 4

Project	Activity
News	Messages
"	Chit-Chat
SR	Index

Fig 5.1: Four examples of access to several Projects
during a single session

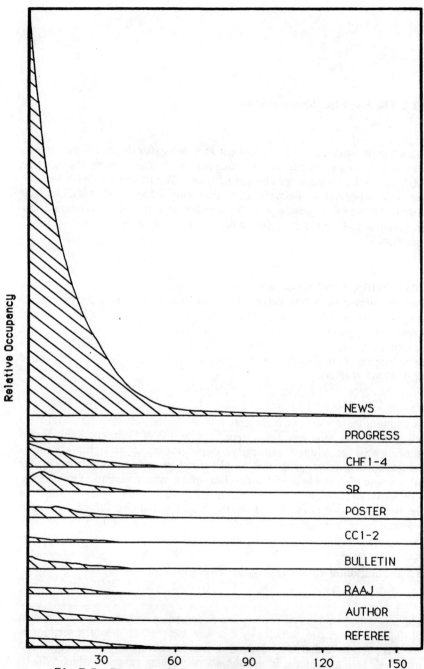

Fig 5.2: The relative numbers of users in Projects as a function of time (in mins.) after log-in

5.2.2 The Need for Improvements

In a telephone survey that was carried out 35 months after the start of the Project, the 32 LINC users, while making suggestions on improvement, often made reference to the program for changing Project. The reason for this is that the use of the program had, from the users' viewpoint, added another level into the system. Hence the sequence of levels, together with operations required, now appeared as in Figure 5.3 - a figure derived from sketches provided by LINC members.

The NOTEPAD system had been designed for people to make use of just one Project entering the terminal type, etc. only once and with the location of all new information immediately referenced by asterisks. Altering the level of interaction required a repetition of this initialisation information and gave rise to some complaints by ten users who would have preferred this initialisation also to be lifted in level. The reasons why this was not possible has been explained in previous chapters.

In addition there were six comments relating to the fact that the NOTEPAD teleconferencing suite was not designed for the job of electronic journals and hence was proving "generally cumbersome", and that Project compartmentalisation means that people report getting confused because they are not sure what is where (4 people). If a similar system were to be used again, a preferred structure would be as shown in Figure 5.4. Here it can be seen that the personal log-in is removed from the loop for changing Projects, and that information on new messages, articles, etc. is lifted up one level.

5.3 Evaluation of the Programs for Reading

The use of the programs for reading was discretionary and, therefore, the amount of time spent accessing articles by this way, the manner in which sections of text were accessed, and the commands given, all reflect on their usefulness and usability. This assessment is the subject of ongoing research which will be published in one of the later reports in this series. Preliminary data would suggest that this additional software was used with increasing frequency as the project

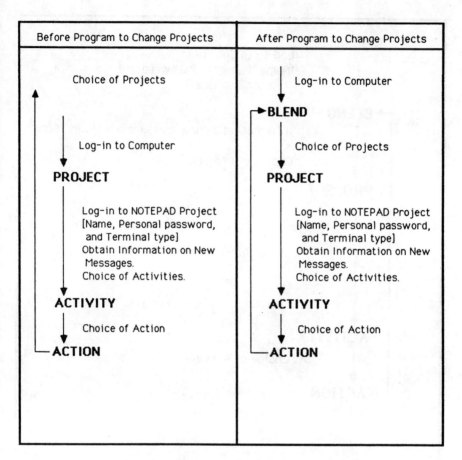

Before Program to Change Projects	After Program to Change Projects
Choice of Projects	Log-in to Computer
	BLEND
Log-in to Computer	Choice of Projects
PROJECT	**PROJECT**
Log-in to NOTEPAD Project [Name, Personal password, and Terminal type] Obtain Information on New Messages. Choice of Activities.	Log-in to NOTEPAD Project [Name, Personal password, and Terminal type] Obtain Information on New Messages. Choice of Activities.
ACTIVITY	**ACTIVITY**
Choice of Action	Choice of Action
ACTION	**ACTION**

Fig 5.3: The structure of BLEND before and after the introduction of the program allowing the user to change projects

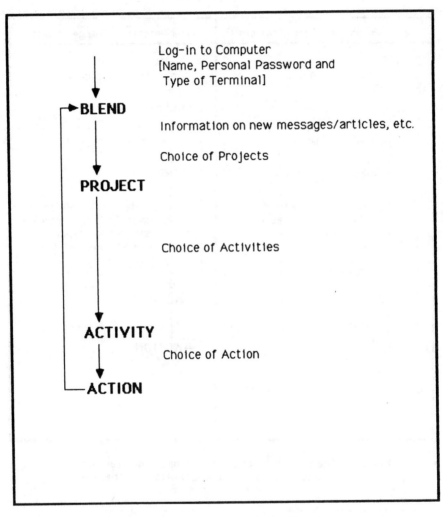

Fig 5.4: A preferred structure for allowing the user to change projects

progressed. This might either be the result of migration by the original members of the community or be the initial choice of those members joining he community at a later stage.

5.3.1 Strategies for Reading Text

As described in earlier chapters, the programs for reading provided for the first time a means whereby the reader might jump about the text. This facility was indeed used in this manner and Figures 5.5a to 5.5d describe some examples of observed behaviour with hypothesised strategies. These examples were taken from the Computer Human Factors section and were recorded by the program for collecting data for evaluation.

The different strategies require different commands and this was reflected in the type of command used. For a largely sequential reading (Figure 5.5a) the reader stepped through the article using the Return key or 'F' for Forward. The reader accessing the results and figures in the article described in Figure 5.5b used the character search string command e.g. "results" and "figure" followed by " to give repetition. Jumping to different sections in the example in Figure 5.5d was largely accomplished by use of the command giving the Entry number to access the section and Contents and stepping through using the Return key or F. The example in Figure 5.5c, although only nine steps, shows the use of all commands except giving the Entry number.

It was clear that the readers of *Computer Human Factors* made use of the flexibility to skip around the text and used appropriate commands to do so.

5.3.2 Possible Further Improvements

In an experimental programme of associated research using the BLEND system, various aspects of reading articles on-screen were studied, including the use of the program under investigation here (Hills, Hull & Pullinger, 1983; Pullinger & Wellavize, 1984). This research suggested one further modification. In the Hills et al. study, subjects had indicated that they might like a fast scroll facility

Article size :   51 Entries

Time to read :   8m 29s

Order of reading

Entry Number	Contents of Entry
1	
2	Contents
6	[Summary & Introduction skipped]
7	
8	
↓	
51	Author's Address
48 steps	

Hypothesised Strategy :

To skip the Summary and Introduction, but to read the rest
sequentially and completely

**Fig 5.5a: Example 1 of users' strategy for reading articles
on BLEND**

Article size : 50 Entries

Time to read : 4m 0s

Order of reading

Entry Number	Contents of Entry
1	
2	Contents
3	Summary
24	Results & Discussion
25	ditto
26	Reference to Figure 4
28	Figure 4
31	Figure 5
32	Reference to Figure 6
33	Figure 6
34	Reference to Figure 7
35	Figure 7

12 steps

Hypothesised Strategy :

To read the Summary, start reading "interesting" result but give up (not all of the text in this section was read); then just step through figures instead, receiving text references to figures unintentionally.

Fig 5.5b: Example 2 of users' strategy for reading articles on BLEND

Article size :   45 Entries

Time to read :   7m 10s

Order of reading

Entry Number	Contents of Entry
2	Contents
3	Summary
36	Conclusions
3	Summary
4	Introduction
5	ditto
6	ditto
6	ditto
9 steps	

Hypothesised Strategy :

To read the Summary and Conclusions first, then start on remainder of text; decide it is not of interest after the Introduction.
[Entry 6 was probably re-read because it is longer than 1 screen.]

Fig 5.5c: Example 3 of users' strategy for reading articles on BLEND

```
Article size :    47 Entries

Time to read :   4m 29s

Order of reading

    Entry Number            Contents of Entry

         1
         2                  Contents
         1                  Title
        47                  Author's address
         2                  Contents
        23                  Overview of progress
        24                        ditto
         2                  Contents
         9                  Aims of study
        10                        ditto
        11                  Next section
         2                  Contents
        43                  Conclusions
        44                  References
    ─────────────
    14 steps
```

Hypothesised Strategy :

Find out where the interesting bits are by returning to Contents and
finding the Entry number; once at the section of interest, step
through it until reach the next section, or have remembered how
many Entries to read from the Contents

**Fig 5.5d: Example 4 of users' strategy for reading articles
on BLEND**

as an addition to the program. Pullinger & Wellavize's experiment showed that a fast page flick as an addition to the program was indeed preferred, and the program could be improved by making this a standard feature.

5.4 Programs developed for System Administration

This section presents a summary of those programs developed at Birmingham without which the editorial processing of text would have been severely constrained or impossible.

In addition to the main aids for the general user, a set of management and editorial aids has been provided. These are principally to cover the inadequacies of the NOTEPAD file-handling facilities, which were created for use in computer conferencing, not for an electronic journal. The electronic journal required much more sophisticated file-handling facilities, especially since the BLEND files had to be structured, i.e. they had to contain the information indicating where the Entries started and ended. This structure was included in the NOTEPAD software by Infomedia Corporation at the request of the BLEND team. There follows a brief description of the management aids.

ADE - A simple line editor.

APPEND - A facility used to append one BLEND file to another while maintaining the Entry structure within the resulting file. Standard system software does not necessarily maintain BLEND file structures.

ASSOCIATE - Used by an editorial assistant to associate a file (containing the text of an article) with a given Activity. Once this has been performed the reading, browsing and refereeing programs can be used with that Activity.

CATALOGUE - A file lister. Used to list files created by the user within a Project.

CHEDIT - Provides the user with a choice of line editors.

CLEAN - A facility to clean out unwanted control characters from a file. When files are transmitted over the telephone network there are sometimes errors due to line noise. This facility cleans out some of the more obvious ones.

COPY - A file copier. This makes a copy of a file in another Project. As a side effect it also tells the user the number of lines and Entries in the file. This was needed as no such facility was provided in NOTEPAD as it was not anticipated that a community would use more than one Project.

DISPLAY - Used to display a file on the screen after it has been transmitted from a micro (for the user to ensure that it is all there.)

EM - A line editor similar in function to the UNIX (TM) editor EM.

ENTRY NUMBER - Used to insert Entry numbers into a file which is separated into Entries. This automatic Entry numbering is used when a file has been prepared for a paper without any Entry numbers in.

PHOTO - Takes a copy of all BLEND transactions that appear on the screen and puts it on a file. This was used to record some of the management actions in case it was required to review them.

QUERY ACTIVITY NUMBER - Reports the Activity number of the current Activity so that Activity files can be matched with their associated Activities.

QUERY PROJECT NUMBER - Reports the Project number of the current Project so that records can be tied to the appropriate Project.

REMOVE BLANK LINES - Removes all blank lines in a file. This is used to tidy up a file as there are many circumstances where blank lines are introduced but are unwanted.

SCHEDULER - Reports on the University of Birmingham DEC2060 schedule status. This gives information on the current priority of the user with respect to other users.

SEND - Used to receive a file which is being sent from a microcomputer. (Special version also written for TORCH microcomputer.)

SEPARATE - Separate a file into Entries. Some micro-computer editors are not capable of handling the file structure of a BLEND file (owing to the embedded control characters.) This utility converts a simple marked-up version of the file into its full file structure.

SET UP FILES - Used on files associated with the browsing facility. Every access word line starting with a * in a RAAJ file gets an Entry number put after it.

SINGLE SPACE - Takes a double spaced text file and converts it into a single spaced file. This was found necessary if the file transfer software a user had on his or her microcomputer was not compatible with that on the DEC2060. Occasionally the file would appear on the DEC2060 as double-spaced.

SPLIT FILES - Used in setting up the RAAJ Entry and annotation files. This utility takes a marked up version of annotations and Entries and converts it into a form suitable for the RAAJ.

TRANSMIT - A file transmission facility, used to send files to microcomputers using Xon-Xoff protocol.

WRITE MESSAGE - Displays a message on the terminal. This was used to send system status information to users before they used BLEND.

6. SYSTEM ADMINISTRATION AND STATISTICS

Martin (1975, p.19) defines a database as 'a collection of interrelated data. . .' In this sense an electronic journal is a data base as the data it contains is interrelated. The software that provides access to the database is the database management system and the BLEND system software forms the database management system for the BLEND data base. To maintain a global view of all the data a data administrator is required, and this task was a fundamental part of the BLEND Programme. This chapter discusses the structure of the BLEND database and the job of the database administrator, especially the methods used in the BLEND system to achieve security, privacy and integrity of the journals. The BLEND system has a devolved administration, i.e. some of the high-level tasks can be delegated to people other than the database administrator. The final section presents some information about the size of the BLEND database.

6.1 The BLEND data-base

The BLEND database has a certain complexity which can be analysed using the entity-relationship method of data analysis (Howe, 1983). This involves first examining the entities that exist in the system. An entity is a type of object of which there may be many instances in the data. For instance, in a warehouse stock control system the entities 'product', 'supplier' and 'warehouse' might be identified.

Various relationships exist between these entities, for instance a particular product is stored in a particular warehouse, a particular supplier supplies a particular product. These relationships may be one to one, one to many, many to one, or many to many. For instance if each supplier supplies many different products but any one product is only supplied by one supplier then the relationship 'product is supplied by supplier' is many to one. This is the basis of the entity-relationship approach. Entities and relationships also have attributes, for instance a supplier has a name and address. The relationship 'product is supplied by supplier' has the attribute 'price'.

This method of data analysis is intended for use in the early stages of software development during the requirements analysis. It is also useful to examine an existing system in this way, not only to analyse its complexity but also to define it.

The following are some of the entities and relationships that can be identified in the BLEND system.

Entities

* **Project**, such as News or each issue of the Computer Human Factors journal.
* **Activity**, such as Messages in the News Project.
* **Entry**, a public message.
* **Note**, a private message.
* **Comment**, comment on an Entry in RAAJ for instance
* **User**, a registered user of BLEND
* **Community**, a distinct group of users.
* **File**, a computer file containing text

Relationships

* Activity is in a Project (many to one relationship)
* Entry is in an Activity (many to one relationship)
* Note is in an Activity (many to one relationship)
* User is in a community (many to many relationship)
* User wrote an Entry (one to many relationship)
* User wrote a Note (one to many relationship)
* Comment is about an Entry (one to one relationship)
* User received a Note (one to many relationship)
* Community has access to a Project (many to many relationship)
* User has access to a Project (many to many relationship)
* User has access to an Activity (many to many relationship)
* User has read up to Entry number in an Activity (many to many relationship)
* User has read up to Note number in an Activity (many to many relationship)
* User is administrator of Project (one to many relationship)
* User is organiser of Activity (one to many relationship)
* User created an Activity (one to many relationship)
* User created Project (one to many relationship)
* File is in a Project (many to one relationship)

In addition to the above entities and relationships there was a need for further 'pseudo-entities' which are distinct from the real ones, and which the software does not support directly. These have been simulated using the entities that already exist, and have similar relationships.

Pseudo-entities

* **Role**. One of the structures employed in the BLEND system was 'roles'. A role was associated with a task or job. For instance, it was decided to provide an on-line support role called 'HELPER'. The idea was that any user requiring information or help could send a note to this role and anyone who had that role could reply to it. This was achieved by creating a pseudo person called HELPER. Anyone with the role of helper was given the password so that they could log in as if they were that person. Thus users could send a note to the pseudo person and it would be received by one of the users who had taken on that role. Another role that was created was that of Sub-Editor in the RAAJ (Pullinger & Howey, 1984). Anyone wishing to make a comment about an article referenced in RAAJ could do so and address it to Sub-Editor and thus the person taking that role. A Sub-Editor could leave or go on holiday while someone else took over that role without interrupting the flow of information. Similarly an administrative role called 'ADDER' was set up, so that one role would register new users on the system, without this being tied to one person in case he/she was not available at the appropriate time.

* **Paper**. The set of Entries which together form a paper. Because each paragraph of a paper is displayed individually on the screen, it was considered helpful if it could be identified by the name of the Author and the (abbreviated) title of the paper. Since NOTEPAD would only display the author of each Entry a pseudo-user is created such as 'Wright (Skips.and.steps)' for the paper by 'Wright called 'Skips and steps in searching an index.' The paper is prepared and split into Entries of approximately one paragraph long. Someone, usually the journal editor, then enters the system as the pseudo-user and submits the Entries. All Entries then have a running header which contains the author's name and a shortened title.

* **User group**. A group of users from a particular establishment. These were used particularly with the library school community who were permitted only to read the journal, and are simulated by a user with a name representing each group. A pseudo-user is registered with a name like 'Birmingham (Reader)', and the password of this pseudo-user is then distributed to all the users in that group so that any of them can log in. This approach allows a very fluid membership without a heavy administrative burden on the database administrator of registering and de-registering great many users. This system was used with the library school community but is not suitable for a user group who want to exchange individual messages.

All three of these pseudo entities were mapped onto the User entity, and during the course of the experimental programme 415 real user's were registered on the system together with 12 Roles, 33 User groups and 119 Paper titles, perhaps indicating the usefulness of the concept in the management of an electronic journal system.

6.2 Devolved Administration in BLEND

The administrative tasks in BLEND are mainly concerned with creating, deleting, modifying and providing access to the more complex entities. They include creating and deleting Projects and Activities, changing their titles and providing access to them; other tasks are adding and removing users, and changing their personal details and privileges.

The administration in BLEND is devolved, that is to say it is not a centralised system with one database administrator performing all the tasks, but rather the tasks are given out to users. The devolution is based firstly on the precise version of the software to be used, and secondly on the position of a particular user in the Project-Activity hierarchy; this means that users may have different capabilities in different parts of the system.

There are three methods of devolution, program-based, Project-based, and Activity-based.

Program-based devolution

There are three levels of the NOTEPAD software, each version allowing more tasks than the previous one. Each version has its own log-in code, and access to the higher codes is restricted to a limited number of users. As well as these three versions, various administrative functions may be performed from outside the software. This provides a fourth, higher level giving acess to the most powerful commands available.

The lowest level of program (Level 1) gives access to all the basic functions of the BLEND system. The majority of users are restricted to this level.

Level 2 gives the additional capability of creating Activities within the Projects to which the user has access. When creating an Activity, the user can say whether the role of the members of it is to be that of a contributor or an observer (the difference between these roles is that a contributor can write Entries but an observer cannot). The user can also say whether the Activity is to be 'open' or 'assigned', i.e. whether other users will have access to it without being specifically assigned to it or not. In the case of an assigned Activity, its creator can also provide the initial membership list.

Level 3 gives further privileges again; these are all to do with the maintenance of the system. This level gives the ability to inspect and change the attributes, such as name and password, of users within a Project, and also to change their privileges or remove them from that Project. Project and Activity titles can also be changed at this level.

Level 4 is outside the above system, i.e. a user accessing at this level does not use the NOTEPAD software at all. Instead there is a variety of programs which can be used to provide maintenance facilities. Some of these have been written specifically for BLEND, and some are part of the operating system of the DEC2060. The privileges at this level are those of creating and deleting Projects and providing access to these Projects for the various user communities, and also providing log-in codes for each community and for each of the four levels. At this level it is also possible to delete an Activity without the need to have access to it from within the BLEND system.

Thus the four different levels of entry into the system provide four different sets of administrative tasks that can be performed. These are nested, that is to say each is a superset of the previous level. The first release of the software only had three levels, 1, 2 and 4; after Level 3 was introduced in February 1982, it was found that Level 2 was no longer needed, and it was always satisfactory to provide access at Level 3.

Access at Level 4 was retained within the BLEND team but access at Level 3 was devolved to the administrators of some of the communities, for instance FERN and MACE. As a special case this third level of access was also given to the editor of the LINC *Software Reviews* journal for that Project only. This was necessary as he needed to create Activities for new software categories. The editor of the *Computer Human Factors* journal in the LINC and his assistant, and the editor of the *Poster Papers* and the Bulletin journals were also BLEND team members and therefore already had access at the third level.

Project-based Devolution

A user can have a set of privileges within a Project which give additional facilities. These are specific to that user and that Project, and a user with special privileges in one Project may not necessarily have them in another. This is particularly useful if a user has some special role in a particular Project but not in the others.

The first Project-based privileges are the standard ones. These give the normal set of facilities in the BLEND system. The second privilege is that of editor, that is, these users have the ability to edit files and modify entries within a particular Project. For instance, this privilege was used by the editor of the Software Reviews journal to prepare texts and modify Entries placed in the system by mistake, and also to modify contents lists in certain Entries. The other two privileges are those of administrator and account manager. These were put into NOTEPAD to provide roles rather than extra privileges, and were not substantially used in the BLEND programme.

Activity-based Devolution

The third method of devolution is Activity-based. Here the privileges are specific to an individual in a specific Activity; outside that Activity that individual may have no more abilities than anyone else. The majority of users have one of the basic roles of observer or contributor; as mentioned earlier, this being decided by the creator of the Activity, though the role can later be changed by the Activity organiser (see below). In the *Computer Human Factors* journal, the papers were each stored in a particular Activity where the users had the role of observer, thus being able to read the article but not add messages there. Separate Activities were set aside for discussion on these articles and participants here had the role of contributor. The two roles were extremely important in controlling the places where people could have discussion.

A further role is that of Activity editor. This is just like that of a Project editor except that it is based on a single Activity rather than a whole Project, giving the ability to edit files and modify entries.

The final role is that of Activity organiser, which has a set of important tasks associated with it, firstly that of registering new users. It may seem odd that this important ability is available to an Activity organiser, rather than to a Project-based role. This does perhaps show a difference between the philosophy of the original conferencing system, NOTEPAD, and that of the electronic journal system, BLEND, which was based on it. Adding and removing registered users is then an important job of the organiser, but became less important when the concept of open and assigned Activities was introduced. This was because with open Activities all users registered in the Project automatically have access to that Activity without being specifically assigned to it.

The organiser can also inhibit (and possibly subsequently restore) either private or public communication by removing the ability of users to write Notes or Entries. This is equivalent to changing their role from contributor to observer and back again. Removing the ability to communicate privately is, perhaps, more appropriate to conferencing than to electronic journal use.

Finally, the organiser can also delete Entries within the Activity or, indeed, erase the Activity completely. Figure 6.1 summarises the devolved administration in the BLEND system.

		Additional Abilities
Program-based	Level 1 –	None;
	Level 2 –	Creating & Deleting Activities;
	Level 3 –	Inspecting & Changing User Details,
	–	Removing Users,
	–	Modifying the Project & Activity Title;
	Level 4 –	Creating & Deleting Projects
	–	Providing Access to Projects,
	–	Deleting Activities.
Project-based	Standard –	None;
	Editor –	Modifying Entries;
	Administrator –	None;
	Account Manager –	None.
Activity-based	Observer –	None;
	Contributor –	Writing Notes & Entries;
	Editor –	Modifying Entries;
	Organiser –	Register Users,
	–	Giving & Removing Access to Activity,
	–	Inhibiting & Restoring Writing,
	–	Modifying Activity-based Roles,
	–	Deleting Entries, & the Activity.

Fig 6.1:   The devolved administration in BLEND

Use of Devolved Administration in BLEND

Devolution of administration has great advantages. The work load of the data base administrator can be reduced considerably by passing it on to others. Communication lines can be considerably reduced; for instance if a user requests a new Activity from his/her community administrator then there is no need to pass this request to the system administrator, and thus the autonomy of a community can be maintained. It also allows a community to organise its own resources (such as disc memory space). However, there can be problems with devolution of administration. More work has to be put into training the users to whom responsibilities are devolved, there is less control over the whole database by the database administrator and, in the BLEND system, he occasionally lost power by devolving it.

The devolution was used mostly to give communities autonomy. As previously mentioned, in the MACE and FERN communities, for instance, a community administrator was chosen and given the password to a second log in code which gave access to software at the third level (see above). The community administrator could then provide the initial support that was needed and only came back to the database administrator for advice or for the higher command functions.

Activity based devolution was used in the LINC in the AUTHOR Project. Here each author could be given an Activity to work in and was the organiser of that Activity. This allowed the author to add other users to that Activity thus giving them access to his or her own material. Authors also had editor role within that Activity so they were able to change their draft documents in order to get them ready for publication.

To handle a properly devolved administration the data base management software needs to be quite sophisticated. For instance, one of the capabilities that is required is that of passing on to other users those capabilities. This can lead to a recursive argument if taken to its logical conclusion. One solution to this problem has been implemented on the Multics operating system (Madnick & Donovan, 1980). In this system a set of seven 'rings of protection' are used. Each ring has an associated capability level and the capability of each is greater than all those before it. To give a user access to a level, the giver must have access to that level also. This type of devolution could be extended over an electronic journal system so that it was dependent on the position in the data base as well as the user involved.

In summary, a devolved administration was found to be very useful in the BLEND system and was used to give users and communities autonomy in their affairs. The system of devolution was complex and more training and support needed to be given to those users to whom the capabilities were devolved, nevertheless, the usefulness of community and user autonomy outweighed any disadvantages.

6.3 Privacy, Integrity and Security

This section examines issues of privacy, integrity and security in an electronic journal system and looks at how the BLEND system treats them. Privacy is concerned with ensuring that private information is not divulged to people who should not see it. Integrity is concerned with making sure that information is accurate, and security is concerned with making sure that information is not destroyed or stolen. These issues are all important in an electronic journal and it is the job of the database administrator to ensure that they are treated properly.

Privacy

In an electronic journal system, private communications take place between author and editor and between editor and referee as in a refereed hard-copy journal. There may also be communication between editor and sub-editors. In LINC two Activities took place which were private communications within the community. These were general discussions about topics of wide interest to the community in the News and Progress Projects, and the presentation of papers in the form of pre-publication drafts or poster papers. These papers were considered private to the community so that they might include views or ideas that the authors might not yet want to be for general release.

As well as private communication, users may also want privacy to write their own papers and develop their own ideas by themselves. Thus private areas of information must be available for users' personal filing of draft papers etc.

It can be seen that there are three types of privacy here:

  privacy of personal material
  privacy of one-to-one communication
privacy of group communication

This individual-pair-group privacy can be simulated on any computer conferencing system and this was done in the BLEND system as follows.

Individual privacy, to prepare material can be obtained in the users' personal Activities in the AUTHOR Project. Here a user is given an Activity of which he/she is the only member. The NOTEPAD system does not allow anyone, of whatever privilege, except the assigned user to have access to the Entries there. Being the organiser of that Activity, the user can add other users to it to give them access if required. In LINC any user requesting a private Activity was granted it.

One-to-one communication between author and editor, editor and referee or between any pair of users can be obtained by using NOTEPAD's private Notes. Here a message can be sent by one person to a named individual in any Activity accessible to both and is then only available to those two people.

Group communication which is private can be isolated in a single Activity or a set of open Activities within a Project. For example the BLEND management team had a single, assigned Activity which only they had access to, for discussion of matters pertaining to the running of the project but which were private, just as a committee meeting is private. Entries made in that Activity were only available to the specific, assigned membership. LINC as a whole had a *Poster Papers Journal* for presenting material that they might not wish to be available to the general public. This Project was, therefore, restricted to LINC members only whilst the issues of the *Computer Human Factors* Journal were also made available to another community. In the case of the EDITOR and REFEREE Projects, an additional layer of security was added. Entry into these Projects was based on both an additional Project password and registration of the user in the Project.

Thus the BLEND system allows privacy on three different levels, private filing, private mail and group communication.

Integrity

The integrity of a system is concerned with how much users trust it, in other words how sure they are that the information they have is accurate. Sources of inaccuracy in a computer system can arise from software bugs and from deliberate or accidental tampering with the data by users.

In an electronic journal system no messages, discussion or papers must be changed if the integrity of the system is to be preserved, yet the editor and his/her assistants must be able to make small changes to the final copies of the papers before they are released. Likewise, authors should be able to compose and alter papers and referees compose and alter reports to the editor, including any comments tied to particular places in the script. It is necessary, therefore, to have a system which allows different users different privileges to change existing material in different parts of the system.

This was achieved in the BLEND System using the various roles and privileges within the NOTEPAD software. The software allows someone with editor privileges to alter existing Entries by taking a copy in a file, editing it and then replacing the existing Entry. For example, the editorial assistant could make any necessary final changes to the papers before releasing them, but the general user, not having this privilege, could not. Also the papers were set up so that the Activity in which they were held was one in which the general user could not make an Entry and thus the integrity of the refereed papers was maintained.

Users in their own private author Activities were given organiser status and editor privileges within that Activity alone. This meant that they could alter the Entries within their own Activity in order to prepare papers, but this did not compromise the integrity of the rest of the system.

The NOTEPAD software is written in such a way that users cannot make changes to existing data unless specifically given permission to do so. When writing software to aid refereeing of papers it was realised that referees might want to change their comments a number of times, also the editor might wish to reword comments before passing them on to the author (in order to preserve the anonymity of the referee for instance). Thus the comments made about specific Entries using the program REFEREE may be changed at will.

Private Notes written with NOTEPAD cannot be changed by either sender or recipient and so integrity is preserved.

Security

Security of a computer system, apart from its generic meaning covering all aspects of security, specifically refers to the problems of theft and destruction. These aspects are partly covered by privacy and integrity when referring to an electronic information system such as an electronic journal. Theft of articles for republication is possible, just as with a hard-copy journal. Theft of the software can be prevented by normal software protection mechanisms on the mainframe computer.

In the BLEND system, destruction of data, either maliciously or by accident, is prevented. NOTEPAD prevents the users from deleting Entries unless they have managerial privileges. The BLEND system is designed so that when users log into the computer they are connected directly into the system without having access to the files containing data. They are automatically logged off computer when they quit BLEND and this also prevents unauthorised access to the files from outside BLEND.

The security of the whole of the BLEND system is an active protection mechanism based on authorisation by password at a number of different levels. Firstly each community has its own log-in code which is password- protected; secondly for entry into the Projects the users must also give their own personal password; and finally, certain Projects have a Project password for extra security. This three-level system of security may be thought to be excessive, but an elementary risk analysis of an electronic journal shows that, although the financial risk of compromising private messages, etc., may be low, the system integrity, in the eyes of the world, must be high. If an electronic journal's security is compromised then it may well be financially ruinous to the company running it as its popularity will wane.

The need for extra Project passwords as well as individual passwords was felt to be important. Norman, 1983, describes a large number of cases of computer insecurity, many of which were due to human error. Typically users choose easy -to-remember passwords which are also easy to guess. Norman cites one case where an important password was left pinned to a board above the computer terminal. It may well be impossible to prevent users making their passwords available to others; a multi-level password system, however, may prove more secure. Clearly, if a user logs into the system purporting to be another user then the integrity of the system is breached as he/she may write messages appearing to come from someone else. Also privacy is breached as that user may read the other's private messages.

Security of a system must not only be considered from inside but also from outside. In other words, if a user gets out of the BLEND system into the general DEC20 command level then the system must also be resilient to attack.

Firstly, the BLEND system does not normally allow the user to leave without logging out of the computer altogether. There might be occasions when this could happen, for instance, if one of the DEC20 disc drives were to develop a fault. Under these circumstances the user might have access to the files which control the system. To avoid compromising the privacy of the other users, these files are encrypted and made impossible to read by any normal process.

The individual Projects are protected by the DEC20 directory protection mechanism. Thus if a user does manage to leave BLEND and still remain logged in, he/she has no more access to the system than from within NOTEPAD. This is a secondary defence mechanism for extra security. The directory protection mechanism used is for each login-code to have a user group which is the same as the directory group of all the freely accessible Project directories but different from the password-protected and other communities Project directories (see Digital Equipment Corporation, 1980).

The BLEND system therefore maintains privacy, integrity and security adequately for a prototype electronic journal although these aspects need to be considered further for any future electronic journal system.

6.4 Summary statistics and charts.

This section examines the use of BLEND from the point of view of the database, with particular reference to the relative and absolute size of its component parts. The material is presented as a series of charts and graphs. The absolute sizes are always quoted in megabytes, i.e. the amount of disc memory required to store about a million characters. To get these sizes in perspective it should be noted that the Bible contains nearly five million characters. The size of any database is always greater than the size of the text it contains as there is an overhead of the relational data, i.e. the data required to control the relations between all the data items.

Figure 6.2 is a graph showing the total size of the filestore over the last 18 months of the Project. It can be seen that the increase in space was fairly linear over this period with a slight tendency to rise in the later months. This indicates a fairly consistent adding of new material to BLEND over the period. The sudden jump in memory use in the early part of the graph corresponds to a time when a considerable amount of data analysis was performed by the BLEND team at Birmingham. This increased the amount of disc memory used but does not correspond to a marked increase in use by the general user population.

The Centre for Computing and Computer Science allowed the BLEND experiment to increase its usage of the disc memory despite the fact that it is normal practice to allocate fixed amounts. This allowed the communities to keep all their old material, which was extremely useful to them. It would have been incompatible with the philosophy of an electronic journal had old papers been discarded. Old messages in the more informal Projects such as NEWS could have been discarded in order to save space, but this would only have slowed the rate of increase. The implications of this are important for future electronic journals. To have a long-term journal one needs an ever-increasing use of disc memory, so that the computer must be capable of expanding to the anticipated size of disc space needed by the end of its lifetime. Despite the fact that computers are becoming more powerful and capable of handling more data, the amount of material published is also increasing.

The expected size of a database is important when estimating the cost of producing software. Boehm, 1981, estimates that the cost of software production can vary by as much as 22% depending on the amount of the data the software has to handle. For a small amount of data a reduction in cost of 6% can be expected over the nominal cost and for a large amount of data the cost of software production can be expected to be about 16% above the nominal cost. The nominal cost is the expected cost of producing 'average software. The size of the

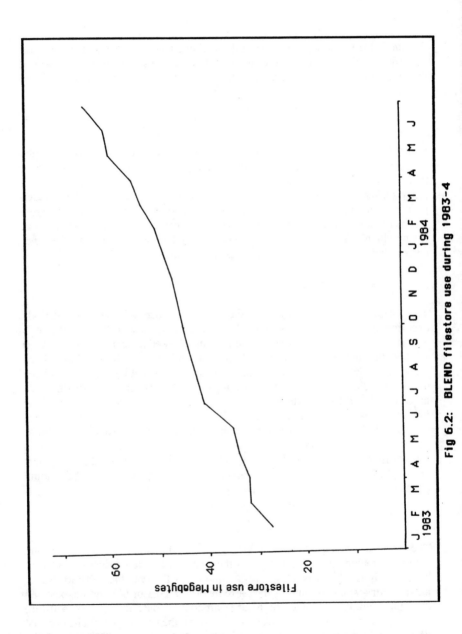

Fig 6.2: BLEND filestore use during 1983-4

BLEND database indicates that the cost of producing an electronic journal system can be expected to be at the top of this spread, that is 16% above the nominal value.

The various communities in the BLEND system normally used different Projects. However, some Projects fell into fell into more than one community's fields and were made available to both. Figure 6.3 shows the different communities and the Projects they used. Various users were members of more than one community. For instance many of the LINC members were also members of the ALVEY community, and many of the BLEND team members were de facto members of more than one community. The software allowed links to be set up from LINC to ALVEY to allow those LINC members registered in ALVEY easy access in the same way as they would access any other Project. Although there was little overlap between the community members and the Projects they used, the fact that there was some, and could be more, made the software far more complicated.

The disc memory usage consists of two separate parts. One is the Projects and Activities which are the main database for BLEND and the other consists of a variety of things which are not directly part of the users' database. This second part contains data stored about the use of the BLEND system. Every time a user does anything, details of what commands were used and how long they took are stored, (although details of the messages themselves are not, in order to maintain privacy). This usage data is considerable after 3 $1/2$ years. There are also the programs which form the BLEND system software, development and test areas and other miscellaneous things. This second part of the total disc memory usage is comparable in size with the main database. Figure 6.4 shows the relative sizes of the LINC database, the other communities' databases and the usage and other miscellaneous data.

Figure 6.5 shows the growth in disc memory use of the LINC Projects. It can be seen that the growth is fairly linear apart from a distinct jump in April 1983. This jump corresponds with the introduction of a set of new Projects including a new issue of the *Computer Human Factors Journal* which includes all the papers in that issue.

Other communities used a comparatively similar amount of disc memory and so they all have been presented on the same graph (figure 6.6). The progress in these communities is quite different from LINC and from each other and so

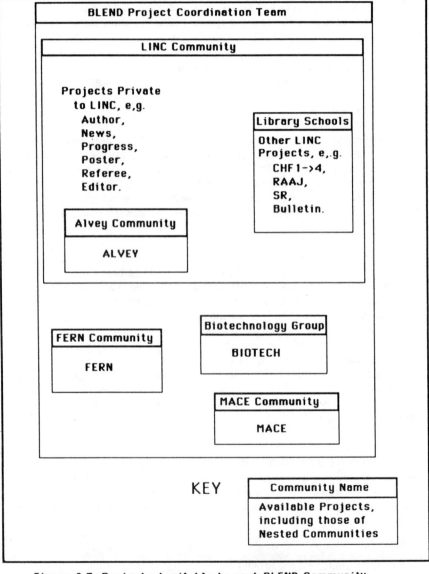

Figure 6.3 Projects Available to each BLEND Community

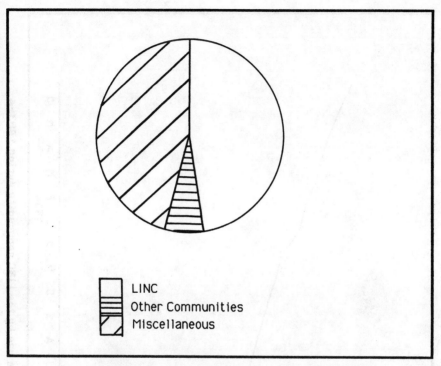

Fig 6.4: Relative sizes of the filestore used by the BLEND communities at June 1984

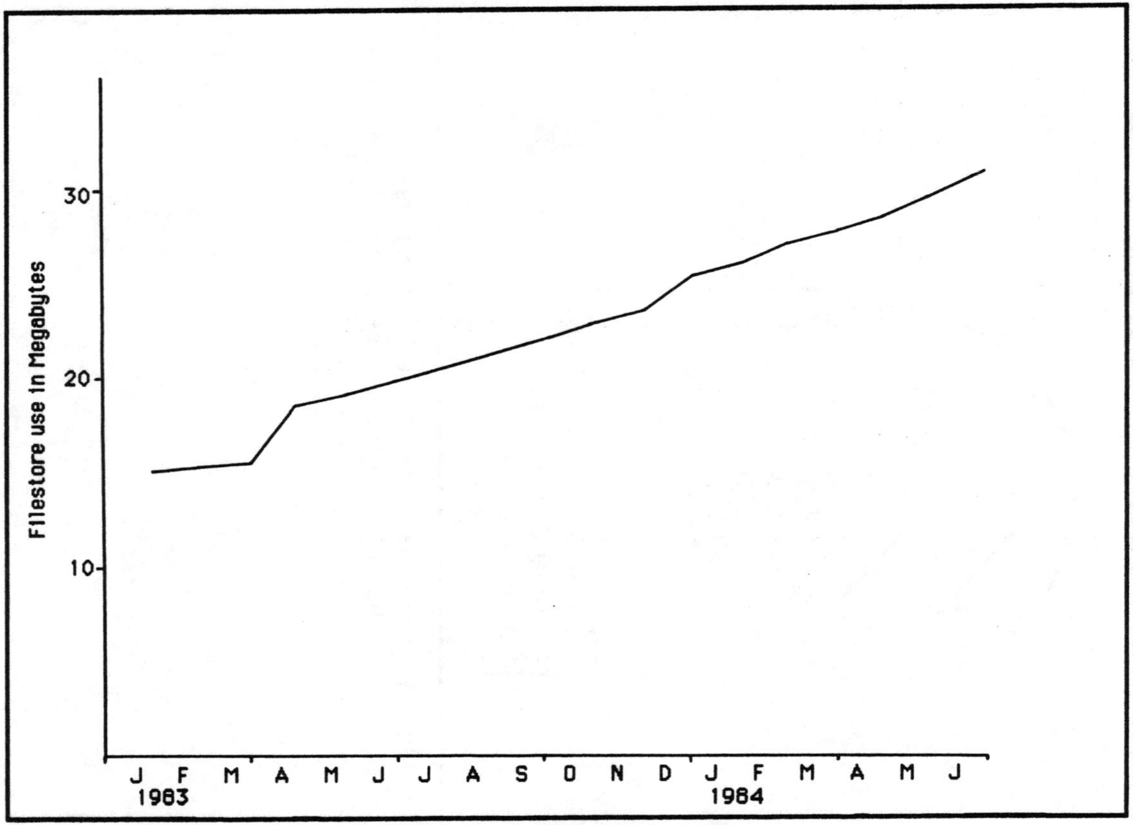

Fig 6.5: Filestore use by the LINC community during 1983-4

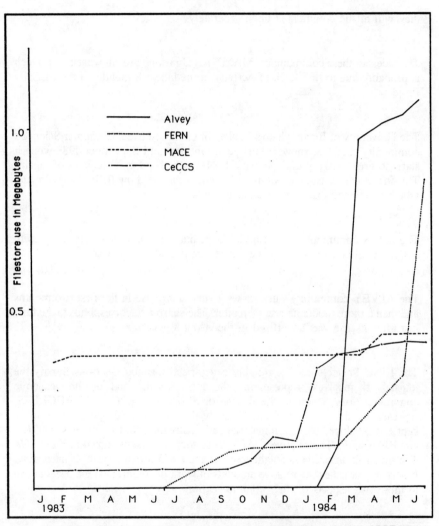

Fig 6.6:   Filestore usage by the other communities during 1983-4

they will all be commented upon separately.

The oldest of these communities, MACE, has almost no growth whatsoever which is probably due to their lack of Activity in the latter 18 months of the BLEND Project.

The University of Birmingham's Centre for Computing and Computer Science's community, CeCCS, shows a fairly constant use until September 1983 when it starts to grow sharply until January 1984 at which point it slackens off again. This increase in use corresponds with courses that used the BLEND system and which conducted exercises in January 1984.

The FERN community has an initial slow, but then increasingly faster, growth as they prepared for starting their community and then did so.

The ALVEY community's use shows a very sharp rise in the first two months and then a more moderate rise thereafter. The sharp rise corresponds to the time just after its use was advertised in the *Alvey Newsletter.*

The LINC Projects may be roughly categorised into four sections. Firstly the journals themselves, representing the more formal end of the academic communication. Secondly the discussion Projects, NEWS and PROGRESS, representing the less formal end. Thirdly the AUTHOR Projects where users kept and developed their own material and finally the editorial Projects EDITOR and REFEREE. The relative sizes of these four sections is shown in Figure 6.7. The similarity in size between the journals and the informal Projects is interesting. It perhaps indicates the relative amounts of work or importance the users attach to these two aspects of their communication.

Looking at the growth of these four areas in figure 6.8 it can be seen that the journals are by far the least linear having considerable variability. This is probably due to the fact that they increase in size when an issue is released or when material becomes available. The dip in use of disc memory in the journals in the later months probably corresponds to a cleaning up operation where redundant material was deleted.

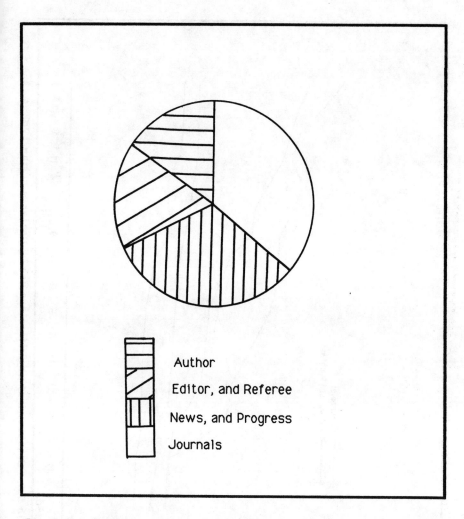

Fig 6.7:   Relative size of the LINC Projects at June 1984

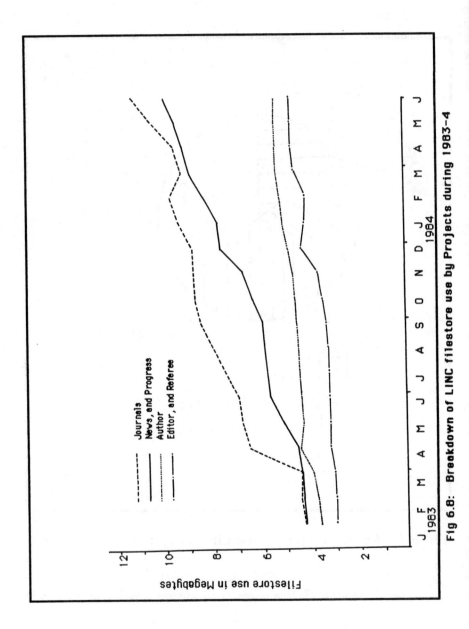

Fig 6.8: Breakdown of LINC filestore use by Projects during 1983-4

The NEWS Project Activities are more different from each other than the Activities of other Projects and so it is important to examine the difference in size of these Activities. Figure 6.9 show the relative sizes of the Activities in NEWS. Here the Messages Activity is far bigger than any of the others, followed by the Teleconference on mail systems.

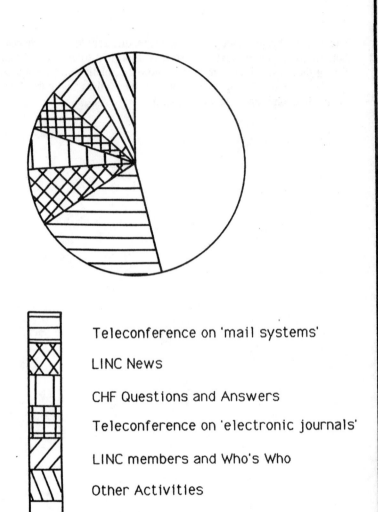

Teleconference on 'mail systems'

LINC News

CHF Questions and Answers

Teleconference on 'electronic journals'

LINC members and Who's Who

Other Activities

Messages

Fig 6.9: Relative size of the Activities in the News Project at June 1984

7. THE BLEND NETWORK

The acronym BLEND stands for Birmingham and Loughborough Electronic Network Development and it is the 'Electronic Network' of BLEND that this chapter examines. BLEND is a centralised system, that is to say all the data is stored in a central computer. To access or add to this data, users must use electronic networks from their offices throughout the world to the DEC 2060 computer at Birmingham. The BLEND experiment made use of existing networks, particularly the telephone network, PSTN, although many other networks were also used. To use a computer system from a distance three things are needed: equipment in the user's workplace, a network, and equipment at the host computer. These three aspects are dealt with in the sections on 'routes to the DEC2060 and 'equipment'. There is a variety of costs associated with using networks; a costing model and a comparison are examined in the final section of this chapter.

7.1 BLEND Communications Structure

Electronic communication systems can be classified into centralised and decentralised systems. Decentralised ones are characterised by the fact that there is no one central machine which is crucial to the whole system. Messages are stored in many machines. To pass messages about they are stored and forwarded on from one machine to another until they reach their destination. The recipient then only has to log into his or her local machine to find these messages at some time after they have been sent. There is always a delay in the message-passing process as the message has to be stored and forwarded between several machines. One example of this type of communication is ARPANET mail based in the United States of America. Another approach, which was adopted in the BLEND system, is that of a centralised computer which handles all the messages. Users have to log in to a distant machine and then send and receive messages on that machine. There is no delay on this type of system as the message can be put in its place immediately. An example of such a system is Telecom Gold's electronic mail service.

In an electronic journal system it is important to have a centralised system as it is essentially an archival system with the added feature of message passing. Once a paper has been written and accepted into the journal it must be archived so that anyone requiring to read it may obtain a copy. In a distributed system there is no definitive copy of any document that can be referred to. To understand the importance of this it must be realised how easy it is to change draft documents electronically. Once a document is produced it is very easy to change it when it is in a computer system, and many text editors are widely available to do this. Thus in a distributed system there may be many copies of a document circulating to many people, any of whom may change their own copy in some way. For instance they may throw away all but a few selected paragraphs which they may keep for future reference. In a few years time someone may wish to obtain a copy of a document referred to in another paper. If this document were distributed on a decentralised message system then there would be no easy way of obtaining a definitive copy without there being some doubt as to whether the copy had been modifed or not. The solution is to have a centralised archival system from which people can obtain copies in the knowledge that the contents of the document have not changed. Copies may be distributed from the archive but once a document is archived then there must be no way of changing it. Thus the philosophy in the BLEND system was to use a centralised system to store the papers, allowing users to take copies onto their own machines if they wished.

The BLEND system not only allows the archiving of papers but also the passing of more informal messages. This is an important part of the system, but a part which need not be centralised. There is no requirement that informal messages be archived or that a definitive copy be always available. Despite this fact it is important that users have a single system to use with a single conceptual framework to grasp and so all message passing took place on the same centralised machine.

Once a centralised system has been established, networks have to be made available to access the archive. It was not the aim of the BLEND programme to establish a physical network so existing networks were used. There are a number of networks available, and it was decided to allow users to access BLEND by whatever network was most convenient to them. The various routes used are described in Section 7.2

Users of the BLEND system need both an interactive system and file transfer. The BLEND system software is designed for interactive use, so that users send commands directly to BLEND, which then responds to them. An alternative way that might be envisaged would be to have a different sort of centralised archival system, one that was designed to communicate with computers. A protocol would have to be set up to handle the passing of messages and documents and then implemented on all the users' machines. No such protocol exists, and even if it had done the implementation problems would have been too great for the present programme, so that this option was not considered viable.

Users also need to be able to transfer files from their own machines to BLEND. Although BLEND has facilities for preparing textual material and editing it, some users may well be familiar with the equipment or facilities they have locally, which they may prefer to use. Not only does this spare them from having to learn a new system, which may well be inferior to the one they are used to; it also cuts down on the use of the communication link, which would be a major expense. Because of this, software was written which enabled users to transmit their material to BLEND using Xon- Xoff protocol, a simple file transfer protocol which is in common use. This also enabled users to receive material from the journal which they could then print or read at their leisure.

7.2 Routes to the DEC2060

During the course of the experiment,people have used the BLEND system from the United Kingdom, the United States of America and from Europe. They have used national and international networks including PSTN, PSS, IPSS, Telenet, Transpac, JANET, SERCNET and MIDNET as well as many local area networks in the process. The majority of users are from the United Kingdom and use the telephone network PSTN, but the extent of use, both in physical distance and networks used, is important. No electronic journal system can work adequately unless the maximum number of users have access to it.

7.2.1 PSTN

The Public Switched Telephone Network, PSTN, uses the normal telephone system but instead of sending voice messages along the wires, computer messages are sent instead. When a telephone call is made switches in the telephone network are thrown so that there is a continuous connection between one telephone and another. This connection can be used between a terminal and computer, and at each end there must be a telephone and a modem. A modem is a piece of equipment which translates the digital computer signals into telephone signals at one end and vice versa at the other. Figure 7.1 shows the equipment involved and how it is connected.

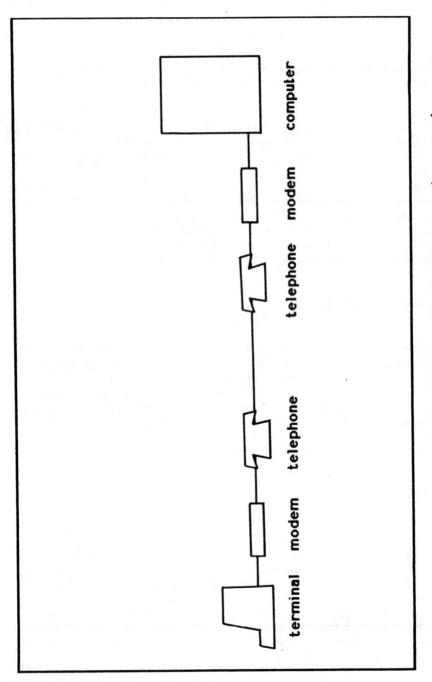

Fig 7.1: Access route using PSTN for connecting to a remote computer

The great advantage of PSTN is that it is simple to use, compared with other networks, and that it is easy to connect a terminal to a computer from anywhere that has a telephone. Users need little training to use the network, and it is well supported by British Telecom. However, it is not cheap [see Section 7.4 for a comparison of costs], although this did not affect many of the BLEND users in LINC, because the BLR&DD grant to Loughborough covered their telephone costs.

Another disadvantage is the line speed, which may be a bottleneck in the system; the maximum number of characters that can be transmitted in a second is typically 30 or 120 [depending on the modem fitted to the telephone].

Pullinger, 1982, reports that a telephone survey carried out after six months' use of the system revealed that about a third of those initially registered had virtually not used BLEND at all. Among the reasons for not using the system was that of delays in installing equipment, such as modems, by British Telecom. This is another disadvantage which may occur with other types of communication.

7.2.2 MIDNET

Another route to the DEC2060 is through the MIDNET. This is a network set up between six of the Midlands universities: Aston, Birmingham, Leicester, Loughborough, Nottingham and Warwick. Computer users at any of these sites can make an indirect link between their own terminals and the DEC2060 at Birmingham. This is done by making a call to establish a link to MIDNET and then entering into a second dialogue to establish a link to the DEC2060. (At the University of Birmingham, of course, users can make a direct, local connection.)

As far as the user is concerned, this method introduces an extra step into the log-in procedure, and another disadvantage is that the echoing of characters is performed by the local computer and does not come from the DEC2060. This may seem a trivial point, but it makes an important difference. If the echo comes locally then any characters typed appear on the screen immediately, whereas an echo from the DEC2060 comes at the point where the software expects the user to type something. Thus with non-local echo one can type ahead, anticipating the prompts that the software will give, and yet the characters will appear in the correct place on the screen. This is not possible with MIDNET. Other disadvantages include the possibility of network congestion, as speed is limited by the speed of access to the local machine, and by the number of users or amount of 'load' on the network.

One of the advantages of this route is cheapness, since for the user the cost is nothing as MIDNET calls are paid for by the universities. However, at the time of the project MIDNET was only available as an experimental service and so was not fully supported. Figure 7.2 shows how a connection can be made through MIDNET.

7.2.3 PSS

PSS stands for Packet Switched Stream and is run by British Telecom. This network is similar to MIDNET except that it is a national network available anywhere in the country.

There are two ways to make a connection to the DEC2060 via PSS. Firstly, a user may have a permanent dataline linking a packet terminal to the nearest PSS exchange. This method operates at speeds of between 2400 and 4800 baud, but the connection and standing charges are high to pay for this permanent link and fast service.

Another method of connecting to PSS is by use of a character terminal. Character terminals are normal terminals and cannot be connected directly into the network because they cannot assemble and disassemble the packets that are essential to the operation of PSS. This job is done by computers called packet assemblers/disassemblers (PADs), situated at packet switching exchanges (PSEs) throughout the country. In this system the user must first establish a link between the character terminal and the PAD, using PSTN or leasing a permanent dataline, then identify him/herself, and finally make the connection from PSS via MIDNET to the DEC2060.

There are problems with this PSS link. The additional network to get through

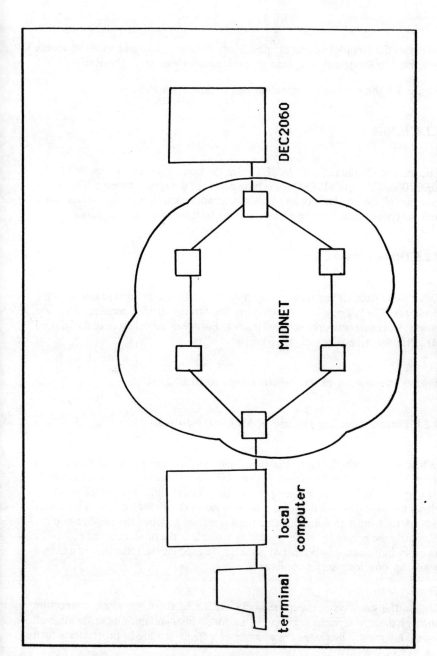

Fig 7.2: Access route using MIDNET for connecting to the DEC2060

increases the complexity and the possibility of error, and again speed of access is limited to the speed of access to the local machine or to the PSE.

Figure 7.3 shows how a connection can be made via PSS.

7.2.4 JANET

The joint academic network JANET is, at the time of writing, connected to the DEC2060 and some BLEND users have accessed the system through this. Again there are all the problems of an additional network such as extra log- in procedure and no type-ahead, but the service is free to those who have access.

7.2.5 Other routes

Other users from abroad have accessed the BLEND system through international networks. The International Packet Switched Stream, IPSS, connects PSS to the North American networks such as Telenet. European users have, similarly, used BLEND via networks such as Transpac.

Figure 7.4 summarises the various routes to BLEND used.

7.2.6 Factors affecting the use of Multiple Networks

When using multiple networks to contact any system there are a series of associated problems. The speed is that of the slowest network. Just as a convoy of ships has to be kept at the speed of the slowest ship, a series of networks slows the user down to that of the slowest network or slowest link. This forms a bottleneck through which all data must pass and so slows the passage of data. Similarly the reliability of the system as a whole is the product of the reliability of every individual component; this can greatly reduce the reliability of a circuit made up of a long series of networks.

Unless the gateways between networks are set to allow automatic connection through them, a separate registration and/or address call must be made for each one. This greatly increases the number of steps in the log-in procedure which

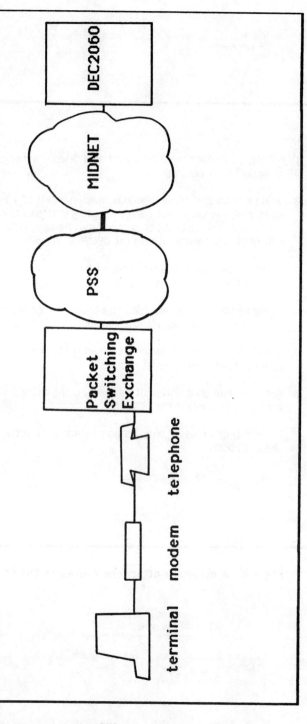

Fig 7.3: Access route using PSS for connecting to the DEC2060

1. Making a call over the public switched telephone network (PSTN) directly to the DEC2060

2. Using a character mode terminal, making a call to a local packet switching exchange (PSE) and then using British Telecom's packet switching service (PSS) to contact the Midlands Universities Network (MIDNET), and then to access the DEC2060 from there.

3. Using a character mode terminal with a permanent data line to the nearest PSE, and then as route 2.

4. Using a packet mode terminal, or a local area network which has a device connect to PSS, and then as route 2.

5. Using international networks, such as IPSS, Transpac, Telenet, to connect to PSS and then as route 2.

6. For other Midlands universities users, using MIDNET via their local computer to contact the DEC2060

7. For Birmingham users only, using a terminal directly connected to the DEC2060.

Fig 7.4: A summary of access routes to the DEC2060

is a considerable burden on the user unless it is carried out automatically using a machine having auto-log-in capabilities.

Networks occasionally send messages to the user with information such as the state of the network. The user has to be able to keep track of all these messages to understand them. There is often no indication of which network the message was sent from or whether it is in response to some other message from the network beyond it.

Another problem of multiple networking is the problem of protocols. For instance one network may expect a line feed at the end of each line and insert a carriage return and another may expect a carriage return and insert a line feed. Thus some connections will result in text being double-spaced and some will have no spacing, each line being printed on top of the next. Some will give a double echo and some none. The user can alter this with appropriate commands to the networks but this requires extra training. As networking standards become more commonly used these problems should be reduced.

Despite this list of problems with multiple networks, there are tremendous advantages as well. The cost of making direct calls using PSTN from abroad might be prohibitively expensive for some and any inconvenience small in comparison. These problems are likely to be transitory in nature if the international telephone system can be given as a precedent. Now telephone calls may be made directly across the world without the user having to make any contact with the network other than the initial dialling. It will not be many years before a similar statement can be made about the computer networks of the world.

7.3 Equipment

In a centralised system such as BLEND there is always a problem of what equipment one must assume that the users have. This applies to both the terminal and the communications equipment. To avoid the problem of forcing people to use certain equipment a minimum standard must be stated and assumed. In the BLEND experiment it was decided at an early stage to assume at least a terminal that could send and receive ASCII characters.

This was the bare minimum that could be workable. With this low standard of equipment there could be no extra facilities, such as graphic material, made generally available. If the experiment were to be repeated now, $3\,^1/_2$ years later, it could be safely assumed that more sophisticated terminals would be generally available and, therefore, could be acceptable as a bare minimum.

It is more difficult to have a bare minimum for communications equipment, allowing users to have better equipment if they wish, since the equipment at the DEC2060 end of the communication has to be compatible. The state of the art at the beginning of the BLEND programme dictated that 300 baud modems be used, that is modems that could transmit and receive characters at either 10 or 30 characters per second. This policy allowed users either to have modems installed by British Telecom or to use acoustic couplers. An acoustic coupler (or to give it its full title, an acoustically coupled modem,) contains a modem but does not need a direct connection through a piece of wire. Once the telephone call is established the handset of the telephone is placed in two cups in the acoustic coupler and the link is then acoustic between the telephone line and the modem.

The modems at the DEC2060 had to be set up to be compatible with those the users were using. Initially a bank of 300 baud modems were used and these were retained throughout the experiment as there were always some users who had equivalent equipment. These modems were linked together so, despite the fact that each had to have a different telephone line, only one telephone number had to be distributed. The users would dial that one number and if it was engaged because another user was using the system at the time the call would be passed on to the next modem and so on. This searching for a free modem is called 'hunting'. The number of modems linked together in this fashion dictates the maximum number of external users a system can have simultaneously.

The problem with the 300 baud modems was that the slow speed of the line formed a bottleneck in the users' communication. There are many people who can read faster than 30 characters per second (about 300 words per minute,) and scanning text can be performed even faster than that. Later in the experimental programme other modems were tested. A 1200 baud modem was installed by British Telecom at both Birmingham and Loughborough in order to obtain a fast link between the two sites. This was found to be extremely error-prone and produced an unacceptable level of noise. ('Noise' on such a communication link means that characters get changed, added or removed at random owing to the equipment and lines being imperfect. All digital communication suffers from this problem but some links are better than others). An alternative modem, used widely in Viewdata systems, operates at a split speed of 1200/75 baud. This works on the principle that, although users might read at a fast speed, their typing speed is much slower. It allows a maximum speed in one direction of 1200 baud and in the other of 75 baud. Thus the user can receive characters at 120 per second and can type them at up to 7 $\frac{1}{2}$ a second. Only those users who have a typing speed of greater than about 75 words per minute are restricted by this limitation which is fast even for a trained typist. Five of these modems were installed at Birmingham, linked together just as for the 300 baud ones. These were found to be acceptable as far as line noise was concerned and were used more by the BLEND users during the later part of the experiment.

During the BLEND programme the Project provided a selection of LINC members with TORCH microcomputers to use as terminals. This machine is a sophisticated microcomputer containing two processors (a Z80 and a 6502), a modem and an auto-dialler. The software supplied allowed the users to log into the BLEND system very simply. The connection between the telephone and the computer can be made using a standard 96A (Prestel) jack socket which can be fitted easily. The microcomputer is simply plugged into this but the connection can be removed when not required. The software in the computer allows the user to select one of a set of numbers previously typed in; it will then use the auto-dialler to mimic the action of dialling a phone number on the telephone dial, wait for the call to be answered by the auto-answerer at Birmingham, make the connection through to the DEC2060 and then automatically log in. The user can, at the press of one or two keys, leave the TORCH to carry out the routine process of connecting to the DEC2060 and logging into BLEND. The TORCH uses 1200/75 baud for its communication and so provides a line with little noise but a reasonable receive speed. This was found to be an excellent way of communicating with the BLEND system.

7.4 Cost of accessing BLEND via various networks

Various routes are available to access the DEC2060 (see Figure 7.4) which use different networks and different ways of accessing these networks. This section presents a comparison of charges for some of these routes. The results give the expected cost per hour of use for various cases, though it should be noted that these figures do not necessarily imply a relative cost of using the different methods since usage time may vary depending on both the route and the speed of transmission. Also the relative ease of access may effect how much the discretionary users of BLEND will use the system. The majority of BLEND

105

users obtained access to the DEC2060 system using either route 1, 2 or 4. Route 4, using a local network, is not examined as data is difficult to collect, we are able to compare the costs for Routes 1, 2 and 3.

7.4.1 Costing models

The cost of using these systems depends on a number of factors. Charges can be either one-off such as connection charges; regular such as rental; or usage charges which depend on how much use is made of the system. To estimate the rate to be paid by various access methods all these must be taken into consideration. One-off charges can be treated in one of two ways; either they can be assumed to be already paid for and thus ignored, or their cost can be spread out over the period of time to be used. Using the latter method it is necessary to decide on the number of years the system is to be used in order to incorporate the cost into the model.

Regular charges are easy to include as the model determines the cost in terms of price per unit of time. The cost must be calculated for a number of different usage patterns, such as half an hour per week, one hour per week etc. When using PSS there is also a charge for data, so that an estimate must be made of how much data will be transferred per unit time on average. To do this it is necessary to collect typical usage data on the number of segments sent and received and the time spent using the system. From this data a description can be built to model the expected transmission. This model may vary depending on the transmission speed used, as transmission rate may affect usage patterns. As a simplification it will be assumed that the number of segments transmitted is proportional to the connect time.

The price of computer terminals, telephone installation and telephone rental is treated as zero in the models presented. It is assumed that users already have telephones connected and paid for anyway which can be used for such a system. Variables to consider are:

the number of years of system usage;
the time per week spent using the system;
the type of call to PSE (local, A, B1 or B);
the type of call to the host computer (local, A, B1 or B);
the charge rate of the telephone call (cheap, standard, peak);
the speed of access (300 or 1200 baud).

Models for routes 1,2 and 3 (Figure 7.4) are presented here.

Route 1: via PSTN

Charges for the individual user are for telephone and modem. One-off charges
are for connection and/or purchase of telephone and modem. Regular charges
may be for telephone and modem. Usage charges are for the use of the telephone.
Here we assume that the user already has a telephone line installed and available
for using with such a system.

Rate for PSTN is

(modem installation[depends on speed])/(time per year x number of years)
+ (modem rental[depends on speed])/(time per year)
+ (unit charge for telephone)/(time allowed per unit charge [depends on distance
to computer and call rate])

Route 2 - Dialling up PSS

There will be a charge for the telephone call to the PSE, and a charge for PSS
usage. The telephone call (PSTN) charges will be similar to route 1. The PSS
charges will include data charge and time charge, network user identity (NUI)
registration and rental.

PSS dial up charge is

(modem installation[depends on speed]+NUI registration)/(time per year
x number of years)
+ (modem rental[depends on speed]+NUI rental)/time per year
+ (unit charge for telephone)/(time allowed per unit charge[depends on distance
to PSE and call rate])
+ Dial up duration rate on PSS[depends on speed]
+ Average segments per hour[depends on speed] x charge per segment

Route 3 - PSS dataline

Here there are no telephone charges, only dataline installation and rental plus usage charges on PSS

PSS dataline charge is

dataline installation [depends on speed]/(time per year x number of years)
+ dataline rental[depends on speed]/time per year
+ dataline duration rate on PSS
+ Average segments per hour[depends on speed] x charge per segment

7.4.2 Comparison

To determine the average number of segments sent per hour the following experiment was performed. Data were collected on typical individuals' use of BLEND over PSS at speeds of 300 baud and 1200/75 baud. From these were calculated the average number of segments sent per hour at the two different speeds over a period of several weeks. The two calculated figures were used in the above models.

The figures obtained from the experiment are:

For 300 baud: 786 segments per hour
For 1200/75 baud: 1184 segments per hour

Owing to the large number of variables involved in the models it would be meaningless to tabulate the results and so a selection of scenarios have been chosen to illustrate the models' working. The models are accurate for any system but the figures for average number of segments per second may vary from application to application and from user to user.

From London the PSE can be contacted with a local call and Birmingham with a Bl rate call. For someone using BLEND for about an hour a week in the afternoons with costs spread over one year the cost per hour would be

Costs in pounds

receive speed	PSTN	dial up PSS	dataline PSS
300	12.08	5.65	20.41
1200	14.68	8.69	29.50

Here the cheapest route is to dial up PSS for either speed.

From Bath the nearest PSE can be contacted with an A rate call and it is B rate call to Birmingham. For someone using BLEND for about half an hour a week in the evening with cost spread over two years the cost per hour would be

Costs in pounds

receive speed	PSTN	dial up PSS	dataline PSS
300	6.68	7.54	36.41
1200	11.18	12.48	51.50

Here the cheapest route is to use PSTN for either speed.

From Aberystwyth the nearest PSE is a B rate call and it is a B rate call to Birmingham. For someone using BLEND for four hours a week in the afternoons with cost spread over one year the cost per hour would be:

Costs in pounds

receive speed	PSTN	dial up PSS	dataline PSS
300	8.34	9.63	5.41
1200	8.99	10.72	7.75

Here the cheapest route is by using PSS dataline for both speeds.

The effect of increased use, both in hours per week and number of years' use, is to reduce the cost per hour on all three methods of access. This is because the one-off and standing costs are spread out over more hours. As PSS dataline has the highest of these charges and dial up PSS the next highest, there is a tendency for the cheapest route to tend towards these two with increased use. In other words PSTN is cheapest when usage is low and PSS dataline cheapest when usage is high.

The effects of distance from the nearest PSE and the host computer at Birmingham has no effect whatsoever on PSS dataline as this route has a distance-independent tariff. The nearer the user is to the PSE in comparison with the host, the more likely it is that dial up PSS will be the cheapest route. Likewise the nearer the user is to the host as compared with the nearest PSE, the more likely it is that PSTN will be the cheapest route. In fact if they are equidistant PSTN is always cheaper than dial up PSS.

The charge rate of the phone call can be cheap, standard or peak. There is a slight tendency for PSTN to be cheapest when the rates are cheap as this route benefits the most. The effect on which route is cheapest is slight as compared with the other methods, especially for the nearer distances.

8. THE FUTURE OF ELECTRONIC JOURNAL SOFTWARE

The BLEND experiment may be regarded as a prototype of an electronic journal system; this applies to both the software and the communities who used it. The purpose of building a prototype is to validate ideas about how a system should work and this 'checking out of ideas' will avoid costly mistakes during the creation of a new system. Therefore an important part of the study was to examine what had been learnt from the experiment and see how this fitted in with future scenarios. This chapter examines some of the issues raised regarding the software used in the BLEND experiment and looks at the future of electronic journal software.

8.1 Communication

Section 7.1 has explained how an electronic journal has to be, by its nature, a centralised system. As described there, the BLEND experiment started on the premise that each user would have some minimum standard of equipment to access this central system. That standard was set at a dumb terminal, that could transmit and receive ASCII characters, and a 300 baud modem. Technology is changing rapidly and this minimum standard could now be thought to be too low. It is possible to buy a microcomputer and modem for a similar price to that of a dumb terminal and modem, and therefore a higher minimum standard of equipment can be expected in the future. Users will tend to acquire microcomputers to use as local workstations on which they can do a great deal of local work independently on the central machine. As more workstations are built with easy telecommunications facilities such as autodial modems, it can be expected that there will be a rise in the use of systems that require use of telecommunications. Such workstations will help users to make connections through networks and this may increase the use of packet switched networks such as PSS.

The use of local workstations will, undoubtedly, increase in the future. In the UK the Computer Board for the Universities and Research Councils has recommended (1984) that degree level students should have access to workstations and that there should be one to every five students. This suggests that they are anticipating people of this level of education having personal workstations as one of the tools of their jobs.

The KOMEX computer conferencing system (Pankoke-Babatz, 1984) provides a virtual workstation for every user, and it is anticipated that these will be replaced by real workstations in the near future. (A virtual workstation gives the user the effect of having one, but the operations are in reality performed by a program running on a shared computer, to which the user has access via a Terminal). This local workstation provides the user with an environment in which to prepare messages and store and organise material sent to them. The user interface and the user agent (a permanently executing programme carrying out certain tasks on behalf of the user) both reside in the workstation and so the communication between user and system is via the local machine only. There is another communication protocol that exists between the workstation and the other machines in the system. KOMEX does not provide a central archive as do other conferencing systems such as NOTEPAD and COM, but the principle of the workstation containing the user agent and user interface will work equally as well in a system with a central archive.

There would have to be a substantial amount of software available on a local workstation. Firstly there would be document preparation facilities; with a text-only system this could be a word processing package. If the journal were to support other media such as graphics then the workstation could also have software to prepare and edit documents in those media. In the near future text and possibly graphics are feasible media to include but in the more distant future voice and video may also be added. The workstation may also have software to aid reading and refereeing of papers. The paper to be read would be downloaded from the central archive and then read at leisure without the need to be concerned about the communication costs although there might be the disadvantage of losing any links or easy reference to other articles in the central archive if this were done. The use of more informal communication such as message passing and the use of navigational aids to move around the system could be in a more interactive mode. The human-computer communication would still take place between the user and the workstation and an entirely different protocol be used for the machine-to-machine communication between the workstation and the central archive.

The BLEND programme made some use of TORCH microcomputers as personal workstations. These have auto-dial modems which meant that BLEND users could have them dial up and make a connection with the central computer using two keystrokes only. The TORCH not only establishes the link to the mainframe but also logs the user into the BLEND system. A more sophisticated machine based on the IBM PC is now marketed by Braid Ltd, and provides automatic dial-up, log-in, message retrieval and log-off. Thus it can be used to collect messages from any central message server without the user needing to learn how to manipulate the user interface, as it can be tailored to any such system. A more sophisticated system has been suggested by Wilson et-al., 1984, called an Active Mailbox. This is intended for use with electronic mail systems and could provide automatic message collection for a number of different mailboxes. It is intended to deal with the problems arising from a large number of messages stored in a large number of mailboxes. It is based on a workstation with access to all these systems providing a single user interface through which the user has access. The same principles could be used with an electronic journal system. The workstation could do all the necessary communication through the network and collect information requested by the user.

In the near future there will still be a need to include a user interface to the electronic journal in the central machine. This is because the machine-to-machine protocols are not yet defined and need to be implemented on all workstations. Therefore it can be anticipated that any electronic journal built in the near future will have two interfaces to the data. One will be a machine-oriented one designed for access by workstations using some machine-to-machine protocol, the other will be a human-oriented one designed for access directly by the users. In the more distant future the second will probably become less and less used.

As more public networks become available and the services they provide better, the use of the PSTN as the carrier network will lessen. If workstations provide a machine-to-machine protocol with which to access the archive then many of the disadvantages of using packet switched networks will vanish. This will also make access easier from abroad.

With the use of microcomputers as communication devices, techniques are available to increase the effective speed of communication. Speeds are limited by the modem, typically 300 or 1200 baud (30 or 120 characters per second). By using text compression techniques the effective speed with which an article can be transmitted can be increased. Huffman coding (see Horowitz & Sahni, 1979) is a very effective method of text compression. It is based on the fact that some letters are used more frequently than others in 'normal' text. These common letters can be given much shorter codes. The normal way of transmitting text is by using ASCII coding, which allows precisely seven bits per character. For some technical texts originally stored in ASCII, compression using Huffman coding has resulted in reductions in size of 35%. In an electronic journal system, if material were to be transmitted in a compact form and then rebuilt in the microcomputer an effective maximum increase in speed of this order of magnitude could be expected. With the reduction of 35% mentioned above, the text could be sent in 65% of the time, increasing the effective maximum speed of a 1200 baud line from 120 characters per second to 182 characters per second. Using more sophisticated methods might increase the effective speed even more than this. Lewis, 1984, suggests that a saving of 50% is possible using a system based on common English words and letters. This would effectively double the speed of transmission were it to be used.

The use of codes may be useful in other areas also. For instance, in transmission of graphical pictures some form of encoding will be needed. For transmission of sensitive material, encryption may be thought to be important. These codes will become more widely used in the future but experimentation is still needed and international standards need to be set. Some early attempts are being made to do this; for instance the North American Presentation Level Protocol Syntax - NAPLPS, (Fleming, 1983) is an attempt to standardise codes for graphics. The data encryption standard and the RSA public key cryptography scheme (Denning, 1982) are both well on the way to becoming firmly accepted standards for encryption. These will increasingly become used as the use of microcomputers and workstations increases.

It can be expected then that in the next generation of electronic journals there will be certain changes in communication and in the distant future more radical changes. Some ideas of what these might be together with the current situation in BLEND are summarised in figure 8.1.

8.2 Electronic Journal Data Structure

The term 'data structure' refers to the way the data in a system is inter-related. The data structure is often thought to be the most fundamental item in an information system since once this is defined, the functions which the software must perform on it are already largely determined. System design methodologies often start with the data structure and then define the software from that (e.g. Jackson, 1975; Howe, 1983). In an electronic journal system there are a number of types of data. The main data structure contains the text of the articles and

	BLEND	Near Future	Distant Future
Network Configuration	Central Archive	Central Archive	Decentralised Archive
User equipment	Dumb terminal	Communicating microcomputer	Workstation
User workspace	Scattered in AUTHOR project & files	Virtual workstation & microcomputer disc store	Workstation disc store
Networks	PSTN	PSTN & PSS	PSS & ISDN
Access speed	300, 1200/75 baud	1200/75 & higher	greater than 1200 baud
User visibility of network	High	Medium	Low
Presentation of material in the network (this is invisible to the users)	ASCII text only	Experimental codes used for increasing effective transmission rates; encryption of sensitive material; transmission of graphical and other 'exotic' material	Standard use of codes for same

Fig 8.1:   A summary of some future developments in telecommunications relevant to the use of electronic journals

messages and their inter-relationships. For instance, if it has articles divided into paragraphs and grouped into issues, as in the BLEND system, then these define some of the relationships.

Already there had been an evolution in the data structure used for electronic journals. The first electronic journal experiment (Sheridan *et al*, 1981) was based on the computer conferencing system EIES. This system has a number of conferences in which there are a series of entries or messages, and can be described as a two-layer tree structure (see figure 8.2).

In the initial BLEND system, NOTEPAD made a more complex data structure possible. The messages, or Entries, were stored within Activities and a set of Activities went together to form a Project (see figure 8.3). Thus this initial system was a three-layer tree structure. However, there was no communication between the Projects and so users could only participate in one Project at a time.

One of the early modifications to the software added a fourth layer to this tree. An additional piece of software was run initially, to provide the user with a choice of Projects. After the user had made this choice, NOTEPAD was executed as a subprocess using the data for the selected Project. After leaving NOTEPAD the user was again given the choice of Projects. This process was repeated until he/she decided to end the session; this was done at the Project choice level. This facility of moving between Projects added a new, fourth layer to the tree structure, (see figure 8.4).

When the refereeing and browsing aids were introduced, a new concept was added to the BLEND system - that of comments which could be attached to particular Entries. These comments were intended to be a value judgement on the content of the Entry, and were attached to the Entries in such a way that the article could be read through without reading the comments, but also they could be read if desired. They were used only in particular places in the system, for example in the RAAJ and REFEREE Projects. Nevertheless this effectively added a fifth layer to the tree structure (see figure 8.5). This fifth layer was different from the other layers. Previously the bulk of the information to be retrieved was always on the the bottom layer. The addition of the fifth meant that the fourth layer still retained the majority of the information but this was not, now, on the bottom layer.

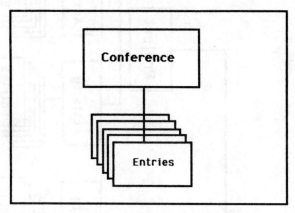

Fig 8.2: The (hypothesised) data structure in
the EIES electronic journal experiment

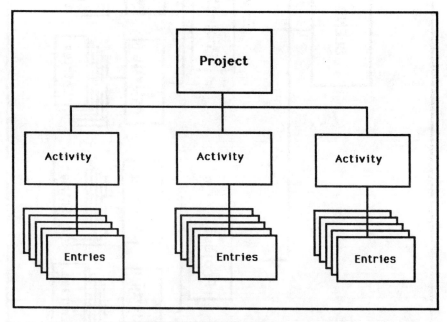

Fig 8.3: The NOTEPAD data structure

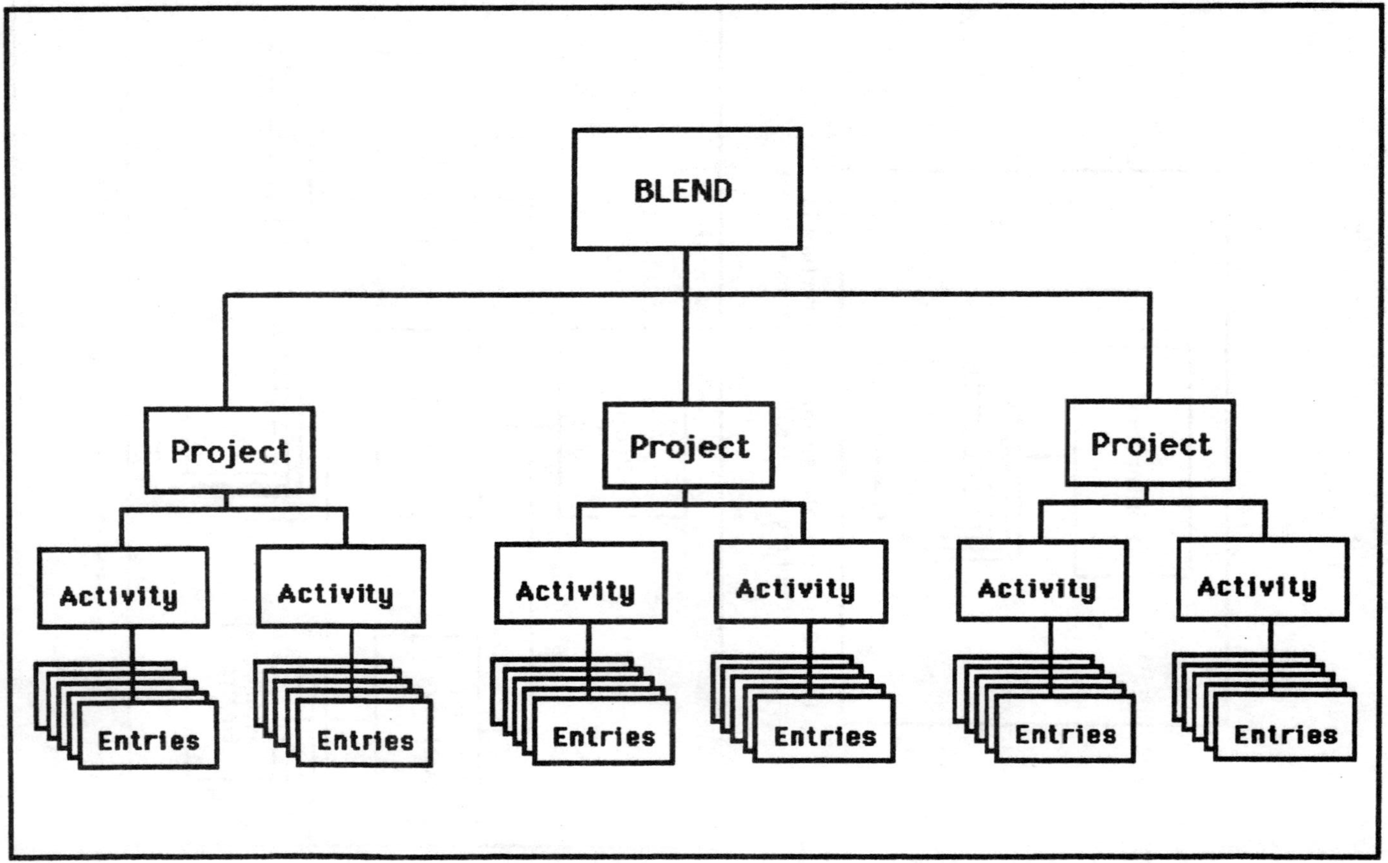

Fig 8.4: The BLEND data Structure

118

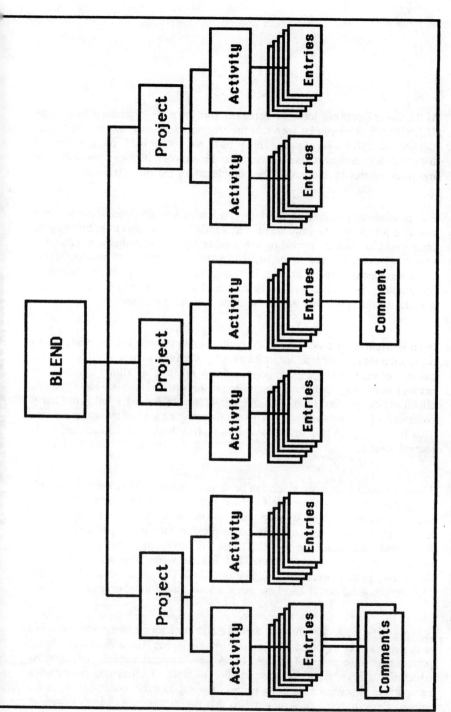

Fig 8.5: The BLEND data structure incorporating Comments

As the use of electronic journals increased from the early experiment to the final BLEND journal, it can be seen that the tree structure used has grown from a two-layer to a five-layer system. This growth has probably been due to the fact that the system designers have seen more and more complexities in the data itself and resolved this by increasing the complexity of the data structure.

It is possible to imagine, in the future, a whole series of electronic journals available which may be implemented as another layer in this tree, this may be categorised by subject, providing yet another layer. The complexity of such a system is potentially vast. In the BLEND system the problem of knowing where one is was identified quite early on. Increasing the number of layers only increases this problem. Human factors testing will need to be done to find out how much complexity the users will be able to cope with in the future.

In an alternative approach, the COM conferencing system (Palme, 1984) is also based on a three-layer tree but includes the powerful structure of 'links', which can be set up between any message and any other. This allows a substantial network of messages which can be related in any desired fashion. Messages can effectively be put into more than one conference by having a link from many conferences to the message and can have comments tied to them by similar linking. This is a very powerful structure and may prove very useful in an electronic journal system.

There are many examples which can be thought of where links would be useful. For instance within a paper itself the text may refer to other parts of the paper such as a figure number. At this point in the text a link could be set up to point to the figure. The access software could provide easy movement from text to figure and back again. In the BLEND-LINC programme the RAAJ Project provided references to other papers, and if these papers were also available on the system, then a direct link could be provided. The comments on RAAJ and the refereeing aid could also have been made using a similar system of links.

Although the basic structure of the BLEND data was a tree, other possible structures can be envisaged. For instance an article may have a far more complex pattern than a linear list of paragraphs. A tree- structured article, or a matrix-structured article, could be created. For instance if an article presented a comparison of several different aspects of several different systems then, in the printed form, it could be structured so that it either presented each system in turn or compared each aspect in turn. The same article, in the electronic form, could be presented as a matrix of sections (i.e. systems by aspects) and the reader could browse in whatever order he/she desired.

An analysis of the usage data showed that around 75% of the time the LINC users spent using BLEND was in the NEWS Projects. This begs the question - should users be put first into the NEWS Project without the choice to go anywhere else until they leave it? This cannot be answered simply and the access software may make this question redundant. For instance software might be written so that users had their own particular initial Project to enter if they desired. That Project could be set by each user to satisfy his/her own needs. Another possibility also arises, i.e. that of having the most commonly accessed material towards the top of the tree structure. This moves away from the BLEND concept of the bulk of the information being held at the bottom of the tree and the other layers just being represented by a series of choices. Extending the idea of a user-definable, individual start-up Project, one can conceive of a system in which the entire structure is defined by each individual user as he/she sees fit. A default structure could be provided, but users could alter their own view of the structure if they so wished. This concept is certainly possible to implement, but it would probably be a major task to do so. The problems of support of such a system are also large. For instance, how does one answer a query on the data structure without understanding the reasons why a user chose to structure it in that way. However, despite the problems this is an important idea to consider.

8.3 The Role Structure

In any communication system it is important to have some 'structures' available. Structures (Wilson, 1984) are best described by examining some of the structures employed in the non-electronic world. A newsletter, for instance, has an editor, a period of publication and a circulation list. These provide a structure or framework which defines how the newsletter will be created and distributed. In an electronic information system structures may be employed which are either specified by the software or agreed upon by the participants and then used by them when necessary. For example, in the BLEND experiment the information had structure in that it was split up into Projects and activities; the software made it impossible to do otherwise. An additional structure was employed within an on-line conference which was set up for a period of a few weeks; a date was set at which to close the conference and an Activity set aside for the discussion. The date at which the conference ended was an unenforced structure; it was agreed between the participants and it was then up to them to keep within that structure.

One of the more useful structures is that of 'role', referred to in Chapter 6. Here again there are the intrinsic roles specified by the NOTEPAD software - those of Organiser, Administrator, Contributor etc, and those explicitly introduced to meet the requirements of the electronic journal system - Sub-editor, Helper etc. It is important to have an appropriate role structures in a communication system and this would best be fully integrated into the software.

One use of the role structure may be as a distribution list. When a message has to be sent to a list of people, often stored on a distribution list, all those people fill the same role. For instance, the members of a committee each receive notice of the date of the meeting, minutes etc. which come to them because they have the role of 'committee member'.

There are a number of other functions for which a role can be used. It is often required to send messages in the capacity of a particular role. For instance, the editor of a journal might send a message to an author rejecting a paper. This is sent in the editor's capacity as a journal editor and should be recognised as different from a message sent as a friend for instance. Another use of a role is to receive messages when the message is to be sent to only one person of that role. For instance, an author submitting a paper to a journal writes a letter to an editor. It does not matter which editor it goes to but it should not go to more than one. In an electronic journal the message would go to the first editor to log in; this method was used in BLEND for the Helper and Sub-editor roles described earlier.

The role structure might also be for accounting purposes. If a user has more than one account on a system, each of which is to be used for different purposes, then he/she might wish everything carried out in the capacity of a certain role to be charged to one account and everything else to be charged to another, for instance, everything done as a journal editor to be charged to a journal administration account and everything else to a personal account.

Roles can be used for controlling who does what. Various capabilities could be allocated to various roles. For instance, only the role of data base administrator might have the capabilities to create and delete major structures in the system. This leads on to the possibility of roles being attached to certain parts of the system. If the data was tree-structured as in the BLEND system then certain users' roles might only be applicable in certain branches of the tree. For example the journal editor's role might only be applicable in the journal subtrees. Separate communities might have their own database administrator for their own subtree.

If the software readily allowed roles to be created and destroyed there might be quite a few roles active at any point in time. This might well lead to complications for the users as questions might occur to them such as:

Which role am I currently assuming ?
What roles can I take on ?
What roles exist that I can send messages to ?
What capabilities do I have in my current role and position ?
What role do I need to assume to have certain capabilites ?

How much the role structure is used and how these questions are answered are problems that will only be solved with experimentation and human factors testing.

The role concept can be extended to fit into any message system. For instance, Maude et-al., 1984, identified the role of 'absence co-ordinator' which was used in a group working exercise on the BLEND system. This was used to establish when the members of the distributed group were going to be away. Members of the group sent notes to this person to say when they would be away and he produced an absence timetable. This is the sort of function which could very well be taken over by a role structure and could be implemented in any mailbox system.

In conclusion, it is recommended that the role structure be implemented in any future electronic journal system in order to facilitate:

a) sending messages to the editor or any other role that may be identified.
b) distribution lists where a separate Activity is inappropriate.
c) distribution of capabilities to perform certain tasks in the system.

The role structure should be position sensitive, that is the role a user has might depend on the position he/she is in the structure.

This chapter has of necessity been speculative, since many more studies need to be performed before any lasting answers can be given to the questions raised here. However, a substantial part of the BLEND study has been to find out what questions need to be asked, and what options are available for a future electronic journal software system.

REFERENCES

ASIS Bulletin. 1978.
Person-to-person Networks
Human Communication and information exchange via computer. 4,5

AXFORD T.H., BURKHARDT D, DODD W.P., LAFLIN S., PARKYN D.G.
& RAMSAY P. 1979
ATOL: A Simple Language with Powerful Data Structuring Facilities.
SIGPLAN NOTICES, 14(3), 5

BAMFORD H. 1976.
A Concept for Applying Computer Technology to the Publication of Scientific
Journals.
Journal of the Washington Academy of Sciences, 62, 306-314.

BENEST I.D. & JONES G. 1982.
Computer Emulation of Books.
*Proceedings of the International Conference on Man/Machine Systems, 6-9 July
1982.* (IEE Conference Publication No. 212.)

BOLT R.A. 1979.
Spatial Data Management,
Cambridge, Massachusets:
Architecture Machine Group, Massachusetts Institute of Technology.

BROWNE D.P. 1981.
*A Study of the Problems posed by the Man-Computer dialogue of the BLEND
Computer Conferencing System.*
Unpublished M.Sc. Project Dissertation, Loughborough University of
Technology.

COMMISSION OF THE EUROPEAN COMMUNITIES. 1980
The Impact of New Technologies on Publishing.
Proceedings of the Symposium held in Luxembourg, 6-7 November 1979. London,
Munich, New York, Paris: K.G.Saur.

COHILL A.M. & WILLIGES R.C.
HELP Retrieval for Novice Users
In *BLEND-5 : The 'Computer Human Factors' Journal*
London: BLR&DD (to be published).

COLE I. 1981.
The Role of Human Memory in the External Storage and Retrieval of Information.
Unpublished Ph.D. Thesis, Loughborough University of Technology.

COMPUTER BOARD FOR UNIVERSITIES AND RESEARCH COUNCILS.
1983
Report of a working party on Computer Facilities for Teaching in Universities.
London: Computer Board for Universities and Research Councils.

CUFF R. 1980
On Casual Users
International Journal of Man-Machine Studies 12(2), 163-189.

DAMODARAN L. 1981
The Role of User Support.
In Shackel B. (Ed.) *Man-Computer Interaction: Human Factors of Computers and People.*
Sitjhoff and Noordhof, 1981.

DEARNLEY P.A. & MAYHEW P. 1983
In Favour of Systems Prototypes and their Integration into the Systems Development Cycle.
Computer Journal, 26(1), 36-42

DENNING D.E.R. 1982
Cryptography and Data Security
Reading, Massachusetts: Addison-Wesley

DIGITAL EQUIPMENT CORPORATION, 1980
TOPS-20 User's Guide
New Hampshire: DEC Technical Documention Centre.

DODD,W.P. 1980
Prototype Programs. *IEEE Computer,* 13(2), 81

DODD W.P., RAMSAY P., AXFORD T.H. & PARKYN D.G. 1982
A Prototyping Language for Text Processing Applications.
SIGSOFT Software Engineering Notes 7(5), 50

EASON K.D., DAMODARAN L., & STEWART T.F.M. 1974.
*MICA Survey: A Report of a Survey of Man-Computer Interaction in Commercial
Applications.*
SSRC Project Report on Grant HR 1844/1.

FLEMING J. 1983
NAPLPS: A New standard for text and graphics
Byte, 8(2,3,4, & 5) (Feb-May 1983)

GAINES B.R. 1981
The Technology of Interaction-dialogue Programming Rules. *International-
Journal of Man-Machine Studies,* 14(1), 133-150.

GOMAA H. & SCOTT D.B.H. 1981
Prototyping as a Tool in the Specification of User Requirements.
*Proceedings of the 5th International Conference of Software Engineering, San
Diego, California, 1981.*

GRINGAS L. 1976.
Psychological Self-image of the Systems Analyst.
*Proceedings of the 14th Annual Computer and Personnel Research Conference,
Alexandria U.S.A., 29-30 July 1976,* 121-132.

HARRI-AUGSTEIN S., SMITH M. & THOMAS L. 1982.
Reading to Learn.
London: Methuen.

HARTLEY J. & FRASE L.T.
Human and Computer Aids to Writing
In *BLEND-5 : The 'Computer Human Factors' Journal*
London: BLR&DD (to be published).

HILLS P., HULL J. & PULLINGER D. 1983
An Experiment on the Redesign of Journal Articles for On-line-Viewing.
Unpublished report to British National Bibliography Research Fund, April 1983.

HILTZ S.R. 1982.
The Impact of a Computerised Conferencing System on the productivity of Scientific Research Communities.
Behaviour & Information Technology, 1(2) 185-196.

HILTZ S.R. & TUROFF M. 1978.
The Network Nation: Human Communication via Computer.
Reading, Massachusetts: Addison-Wesley.

HOROWITZ E. & SAHNI S. 1979
Fundamentals of Computer Algorithms.
London: Pitman

HOWE D.R. 1983
Data Analysis for Data Base Design.
London: Arnold, 1983.

JACKSON M.A. 1975
Principles of Program Design,
London: Academic Press.

JOHANSEN R., VALLEE J., & SPANGLER K. 1979.
Electronic Meetings: Technical Alternatives and Social Choices.
Reading, Massachusetts: Addison-Wesley.

LANCASTER F.W. 1978
Towards Paperless Information Systems
New York: Academic Press.

LEWIS M. 1984
A Quart in a Pint Pot.
Practical Computing, 7(6), 47-49

MADNICK S.E. & DONOVAN J.J. 1980
Operating Systems
New York: McGraw-Hill

MAGUIRE M. 1982.
Computer Recognition of Textual Keyboard Inputs from Naive Users.
Behaviour & Information Technology, 1(1), 93-111.

MARTIN J. 1975
Computer Database Organisation
New Jersey: Prentice Hall.

MAUDE T., DODD W.P., PULLINGER D., & SHACKEL B. 1982
The BLEND Electronic Journal System.
IUCC Bulletin, 5(1), 22-26.

MAUDE T.I. & DODD W.P. 1985
A Rapid Prototyping Case Study.
Proceedings of the 8th International Computing Symposium (Computing '85)
Florence, Italy,
(March 1985), (Eds: Bucci, G., & Valle, G.); Amsterdam: North Holland

MAUDE T.I., HEATON N.O., GILBERT G.N., WILSON P.A. & MARSHALL C.J. 1984
An Experiment in Group Working on Mailbox Systems
Proceedings of the 1st International Conference on Computer Human Interaction (INTERACT '84), London, 1984.

MEADOWS A.J. 1980
New Technology and Developments in the Communication of Research during the 1980's
Leicester University Primary Communication Research Centre Occasional Paper, BLR&DD Report 5562.

MILLER D.P. 1981.
The Depth-Breadth Trade-off in Hierarchical Computer Menus.
Proceedings of the 25th Annual Conference of the Human Factors-Society. 296-300.

MORRISON D.L. & GREEN T.R.G.
Adaptive Interface Techniques in Recognising Speed and Similar Inputs
In *BLEND-5 : The 'Computer Human Factors' Journal*
London: BLR&DD (to be published).

NORMAN A.R.D. 1983
Computer Insecurity
London: Chapman & Hall 1983.

PALME J. 1984
A Survey of Computer Based Message Systems
Proceedings of the 1st International Conference on Human-Computer (INTERACT '84), London, 1984

PALME J. & ENDERIN L.
COM Teleconferencing System - Concise Manual.
(FOA Report No. C10129E-M6(ES).
Stockholm: Swedish National Defence Research Institute.

PANKOKE-BABATZ, U. 1984
The Computer Conferencing System KOMEX
Proceedings of the 1st International Conference on Computer Human Interaction (INTERACT '84), London, 1984

PULLINGER, D.J. 1982.
6-Month Phone Survey of the LINC Community on BLEND - A Short Factual Account.
(HUSAT Memo No.258).
Loughborough University of Technology U.K: Dept.of Human Sciences.

PULLINGER D.J. 1983a
Enhancing NOTEPAD Teleconferencing for the BLEND 'Electronic Journal'.
Loughborough University of Technology, U.K: Dept. of Human Sciences.
(HUSAT Memo. No.284).

PULLINGER D.J. 1983b
Attitudes to traditional journal procedure.
Electronic Publishing Review, 3(3), 213-222.

PULLINGER D.J. 1983c
BLEND User's Guide.
Loughborough University of Technology, U.K: Dept. of Human Sciences.

PULLINGER D.J. & HOWEY K. 1984
The Development of the Reference, Abstract & Annotations Journal (RAAJ) on the BLEND System.
Journal of Librarianship, 16(1), 19-33.

PULLINGER D., SHACKEL B., DODD W.P. & MAUDE T.I. 1984 User Surveys in the BLEND-LINC 'electronic journal' project. *Proceedings of the 1st-International Conference on Computer Human Interaction (INTERACT '84), London, 1984*

PULLINGER D. & WELLAVIZE D. 1984
An Experiment into Reading Journal Articles on Screen
Unpublished report to the British National Bibliography Research Fund,
September 1984.

ROYAL SOCIETY. 1981.
A Study of the Scientific Information System in the United Kingdom.
London: British Library and Royal Society. British Library Research &
Development Report No.5626.

SENDERS, J. 1977.
An On-line Scientific Journal.
The Information Scientist, 11(1), 3-9

SHACKEL B. 1982
The BLEND System Programme for the Study of some Electronic Journals.
Computer Journal 25(2), 161-168 and *Ergonomics* 25(4), 269-284.

SHACKEL B. 1983
"The BLEND system Layout of Papers for LINC" Manual.
Loughborough University of Technology, U.K.: Dept.of Human Sciences.

SHACKEL B., PULLINGER D.J., MAUDE T.I., DODD W.P. 1983
The BLEND-LINC Project on 'Electronic Journals' after Two Years.
ASLIB Proceedings 35(2), 77; and *Computer Journal* 26(3), 247-254.

SHERIDAN T., SENDERS J., MORAY N., STOKLOSA J., GUILAUME J.,
& MAKEPEACE D. 1981.
*Experimentation with a Multi-disciplinary Teleconference and Electronic Journal
on Mental Workload.*
Unpublished report to National Science Foundation (Division of Science
Information Access Improvement) 320 pp. Available from Prof. T. Sheridan,
Room 1-110, M.I.T., Cambridge, Mass. 02139.

SPENCE R. and APPERLEY, M. 1982.
Database Navigation: an Office Environment for the Professional.
Behaviour & Information Technology 1(1), 43-54.

TANENBAUM A.S. 1981.
Network Protocols
Computing Surveys 13(4).

UHLIG R.P. (Ed.). 1981.
Computer Message Systems.
Proceedings of the IFIP TC-6 International Symposium on Computer Message Systems, Ottawa, Canada 6-8 April 1981. North-Holland Pub. Co.

VALLEE J. 1984.
Computer Message Systems
New York: McGraw Hill.

VALLEE J. & WILSON T. 1976.
Computer Based Communication in Support of Scientific and Technical Work.
NASA Report CR 137879.

VAN NES F.C. and VAN DER HEIJDEN J. 1980.
Data Retrieval with Hierarchical or Direct Entry Methods.
Talk presented to the Ergonomics Society Conference, Nottingham.

WILSON P.A. 1984
Structures for Mailbox Systems Applications
Proceedings of the IFIP 6.5 Working Conference on Computer Message Services Nottingham, U.K., 1-4 May 1984

WILSON P.A., MAUDE T.I., MARSHALL C.J. & HEATON N. 1984
The Active Mailbox - your on-line secretary.
Proceedings of the IFIP 6.5 Working Conference on Computer Message Services, Nottingham, U.K., May 1984.

WOODWARD A. 1976.
Editorial Processing Centres: Scope in the United Kingdom.
London: British Library (British Library Research & Development Report No.5271).

WOODWARD A.M., YSKA G. & MARTYN J. 1976.
The Applicability of Editorial Processing Centres to UK Scholarly Publishing.
London:
British Library (British Library Research & Development Report No. 5270)

GLOSSARY

Action
Inside all Activities there are 9 principal operations that can be commanded by the user; these have been mapped onto the digits 1 to 9 for ease of use and are called Actions.

Activity
An Activity is a meeting area with named participants.

Activity Organiser
This person has special powers inside an Activity which include being able to add or remove participants as well as to control more closely the material entered.

Administrator
This is the person who has access to the file system of the Project and whose responsibility it is to create Activities and monitor their size and usage. (Also "Account Administrator").

BLEND
Birmingham and Loughborough Electronic Network Development. BLEND is the name of the computer software system mounted on the Birmingham University DEC2060 based on NOTEPAD software (see below).

CHF
The Computer Human Factors journal used by LINC

Contributor
A contributor is a 'standard' named participant of any Activity.

Editor
An editor is a contributor with the added faciltiy of being able to amend public messages by the command REPLACE Entries.

Entry
An Entry is a public message to all the members of an Activity and can be likened to making a statement or asking a question at a conference.

LINC	Loughborough Information Network Community. The particular community of people involved in the experimental programme of scientific communication with various types of electronic journal, and especially with the electronic journal 'Computer Human Factors'.
MIDNET	The Midlands Universities' network, a computer network between six Midland Universities.
NEWS	An informal communication Project used by LINC.
Note	A Note is a private message from sender to recipient and only visible to them.
NOTEPAD	is the name of a software suite which is a proprietary product of the InfoMedia Corporation. This has been bought for the 3 year experimental programme and it has been mounted on the University of Birmingham DEC2060 to form the software basis of the BLEND system.
Observer	An observer is a member of an Activity who is not permitted to make public messages - i.e. who cannot write entries.
POSTER	The Poster Papers Journal used by LINC.
Project	A Project is a security bounded area of BLEND. To enter a Project a person must have previously been made a member by name and must also use a personal passwork. Inside each Project there can be many Activities (see Activity).

PSS	Packet Switched Stream, a U.K. national network set up and run by British Telecom.
PSTN	Public Switched Telephone Network, the telephone system which can be used as a computer network.
RAAJ	The References, Abstracts and Annotations Journal used by LINC.
Role	A user of NOTEPAD has a role assigned to him by the organiser of the Activity. This may be one of the four: Organiser, Editor, Contributor, Observer.
SR	The Software Reviews Journal used by LINC.

OTHER REPORTS

Library and Information Research (LIR) Reports may be purchased from the British Library Publications Sales Unit, Boston Spa, Wetherby, West Yorkshire LS23 7BQ, UK. Details of some other LIR Reports are given below.

LIR Reports 35. Belkin, Nicholas J and Vickery, Alina *Interaction in information systems a review of research from document retrieval to knowledge based systems.* December 1985. pp viii + 250. ISBN 0 7123 3050 X.

The researchers are concerned with the interaction of users with information systems. This includes the interaction of users with skilled intermediaries carrying out searches on their behalf. The report's main focus is on computerised bibliographic systems but it includes a chapter on question answering and expert systems.

LIR Report 36. Craddock, Peter. *The public library and blind people: a survery and reivew of current practice.* December 1985. pp xvi + 106. ISBN 0 7123 3051 8.

A postal questionnaire, visits to libraries and other relevant agencies, and personal contacts contributed to this assessment of the role of public libraries. Few libraries have identified the blind as a target group and the dominant role is one of referral to other agencies. Current trends in information technology and tape services provide incentives for libraries to establish or review policies and become more involved through in-house initiatives and in cooperation with other agencies.

LIR Report 37. Dee, Marianne and Bowen, Judith, *Library services to older people.* February 1986. pp viii + 186. ISBN 0 7123 3056 9.

The report assesses the extent to which public libraries have recognised the needs of older people and have made specific arrangements for them. Services to older people were found to be a priority in about half the library authorities interviewed but emphasis was still on providing collections to residential homes and day centres and on housebound services. Examples of effective use of library resources include thier applications in bibliotherapy, in local clubs and in cooperation with self-help groups.

LIR Report 38. Wells, Rosemary. *Newsplan: report of the pilot project in the South-West.* May 1986. pp x + 218. Section II fiche only. ISBN 0 7123 3057 7.

This report presents the results of a survey on the state of preservation of holdings of newspapers in libraries, museums, archives offices and newspaper offices in the South West library region. Section I includes a history of newspaper production, an account of the holdings of organisations in the region, information on the use of microfilm for newspaper preservation, a statement of the methodology of the project and recommendations. Section II details for every newspaper title its history, the location of sets suitable for microfilming, information on microfilming already done, gaps in the surviving series and future planning of a presentation programme.

LIR Report 39. Mitev, Nathalie Nadia, Venner, Gillian M and Walker, Stephen. *Designing an online public access catalogue: Okapi, a catalogue on a local area network.* August 1985. pp xiv + 254. ISBN 0 7123 3058 5.

The aim was to produce an online public access catalogue (OPAC) on a local area network (LAN), that would be readily usable without training or experience. The result was a functioning prototype OPAC called Okapi, which has a number of distinctive features, such as coloured keys for ease of use, lack of jargon and search decision trees. There is a full description of Okapi under the headings: source file, indexing, search functions, user interaction and evaluation. There are also chapters on OPACs in general, LANs and recommendations for future research.

LIR Report 41. Goldsmith, G and Williams, PW. *Online searching made simple: a microcomputer interface for inexperienced users.* March 1986. pp x + 113. ISBN 0 7123 3059 3.

The authors investigated the feasibility of searching systems for unskilled users and developed a working system on a Superbrain microcomputer. They constructed a program which successfully interviews the user, formulates the search in the chosen search language, and then automatically logs on to the appropriate host and carries out the search.

LIR Report 43. Weeks, Jeffrey. *Family studies — information needs and resources: the report of the Review Panel on Family Studies.* April 1986. pp xii + 123. ISBN 0 7123 3066 6

The report investigates aspects of current information provision and support in a variety of national agencies associated with research and practice in family studies. It describes the contribution of a number of bodies, deals with the dissemination of research findings and the impact of new technology, and makes recommendations for the improved coverage of information services in specialised areas of social policy and research.

LIR Report 44. White, Brenda. *Interlending in the United Kingdom 1985: a survey of interlibrary document transactions.* August 1986. pp xii + 86. ISBN 0 7123 3068 2.

The aim of a survey of interlibrary loans carried out in 1985, and of this report, is to present a national picture of interlibrary lending in the UK and Ireland in 1985, and to compare and contrast it with the national picture revealed in the first survey in 1977. Where appropriate a geographical breakdown is given.

LIR Report 45. Pullinger D J. *BLEND-4: user-system interaction.* December 1985. pp xii + 76. ISBN 0 7123 3070 4.

The author describes the interaction of a group of users with the Birmingham and Loughborough Electronic Network Development (BLEND) system over a four-year experimental period. The users were from the subject area of human-computer interaction, which underwent rapid development during the experiment. How long users spent in each of the informal and formal levels of communication was studied. To aid users substantial effort was made in user support and this is described. Finally the author explained how easy the system was to use and its integration into everyday working life.

LIR Report 47. Shackel, B (editor). *BLEND-5: the Computer Human Factors Journal.* July 1986. pp xii + 221. ISBN 0 7123 3073 9.

The original proposals for the BLEND experimental programme were to test and evaluate the setting up of a refereed papers electronic journal. This report contains the unaltered collection of papers that were reviewed and accepted by the editors for archiving in electronic form only.

LIR Report 48. Slater, M. *Careers guidance and library/information work.* October 1986. pp x + 176. ISBN 0 7123 3076 3.

A qualitative study of the role and activities of UK careers advisers in relation to library/information work was undertaken by Aslib. The study covered both the secondary and tertiary education levels, and the relatively new phenomenon of computer-assisted guidance.

LIR Report 49. Pinion, Catherine. *Legal deposit of non-book materials.* November 1986. pp x + 144. ISBN 0 7123 3077 1.

The author identified and examined the practical problems of legal deposit of non-book materials. As a result of her study it is hoped that it might be possible to identify where the archives were adequate, areas where they would need to be built upon, and areas that could not reasonably be covered by existing legislation.

LIR Report 50. Ernestus, H and Weger, H-D (eds). *Bertelsmann Foundation colloquium — public libraries today and tomorrow: approaches to their goals and management.* December 1986. pp x + 228. ISBN 0 7123 3078 X.

An international colloquium was held in Gütersloh, West Germany in autumn 1984. Topics covered included the role of the library in society, library response to political trends, the goal setting process, marketing, new media, organisational management, cost effectiveness, support by central agencies, funding alternatives for libraries and public relations.

LIR Report 51. Trott, Fiona. *Information for industry: a study of the information needs of small firms and the relevance of public information services.* October 1986. pp xii + 94. ISBN 0 7123 3079 8.

There are sources for business and commercial information available through the public library network, giving the small businessman, in theory, the same access to publicly available information as the large multinational. A pragmatic study, closely monitoring the needs of 43 firms in Suffolk, representing manufacturing and services industries was undertaken. A research officer acquainted a controlled sample of local firms with the range of services available and assessed whether a public library service could meet the needs identified.